AF024

MASSIMILIANO AFIERO

AXIS FORCES 24

WW2 AXIS FORCES

The Axis Forces number 24 – November 2023

Direction and editing: Via San Giorgio, 11 – 80021 AFRAGOLA (NA) -ITALY

Managing and Chief Editor: Massimiliano Afiero

Email: maxafiero@libero.it - **Website:** www.maxafiero.it

Contributors

Tomasz Borowski, Grégory Bouysse, Stefano Canavassi, Carlos Caballero Jurado, Rene Chavez, Gary Costello, Paolo Crippa, Carlo Cucut, Antonio Guerra, John B. Köser, Lars Larsen, Christophe Leguérandais, Eduardo M. Gil Martínez, Michael D. Miller, Peter Mooney, Péter Mujzer, Ken Niewiarowicz, Erik Norling, Raphael Riccio, Marc Rikmenspoel, Guido Ronconi, Hugh Page Taylor, Charles Trang, Sergio Volpe

Editorial

Here we are (finally!) at the third and final issue of this year's magazine. We worked a lot to be able to publish articles of a certain level and above all to deal with topics of great historical and military interest, also helped by the fact of having a higher number of pages than in the past. So continue to follow us in ever-increasing numbers and let us know about themes and topics to be covered in future issues, to better respond to your needs. The greater number of pages gives us the possibility of publishing more in-depth and complete articles and above all accompanied by numerous photos and maps. As always, we will try to deal with new and little-known topics, with particular interest in the voluntary formations of the Axis. Let us now analyze the contents of this new issue of the magazine. We begin with a long and interesting work on the use of the Hitler Youth division on the Normandy front, in the initial phases of the bloody fighting that raged on French soil in the summer of 1944. An article follows on the Italian light tanks, much maligned by official historiography, but which were used on all war fronts, especially as reconnaissance vehicles. We continue with the history of the Totenkopf division, this time dealing with the period between October 1943 and January 1944. We continue the history of the Italian units on the Eastern front, talking about the first battle on the Don and we close with an interesting article on the battle of Monterotondo, which saw German paratroopers engaged after 8 September 1943. Always hoping to have met your interest in military history, I wish everyone happy reading and see you in the next issue.

Massimiliano Afiero

The publication of The Axis Forces deals exclusively with subjects of a historical military nature and is not intended to promote any type of political ideology either present or past, as it also does not seek to exalt any type of political regime of the past century or any form of racism.

Contents

12.SS-Panzer-Division 'Hitlerjugend', Normandy Front	Pag. 5
Italian light tanks CV L3/33-35-38	Pag. 24
The Totenkopf Division on the Eastern Front Oct. 1943 – Jan. 1944	Pag. 32
The Italian 8th Army in Russia, The First Defensive Battle of the Don	Pag. 54
Sprungeinsatz Monterotondo, 9-10 of September, 1943	Pag. 81

12.SS-Panzer-Division 'Hitlerjugend' Normandy Front

by Massimiliano Afiero

The invasion begins

Around midnight on June 5, 1944, news began to arrive at divisional headquarters of paratroopers landing south of the coastal area. The *I.SS-Panzer-Korps*, for its part, did not receive any orders or reports. At approximately 02:30, the division alerted all its units notwithstanding the lack of guidance from above. *SS-Hstuf.* Gerd Freiherr von Reitzenstein, an officer of the *SS-Aufklärungs-Abteilung*, reported: ".... *June 6, 1944. Alert for all units at approximately 02:00. Order to move immediately to the designated points. It was still dark when the Aufklärungs-Abteilung started to move. At around 4:00, the vehicles took up position at selected crossroads, under the protection of the Flak pieces.* "

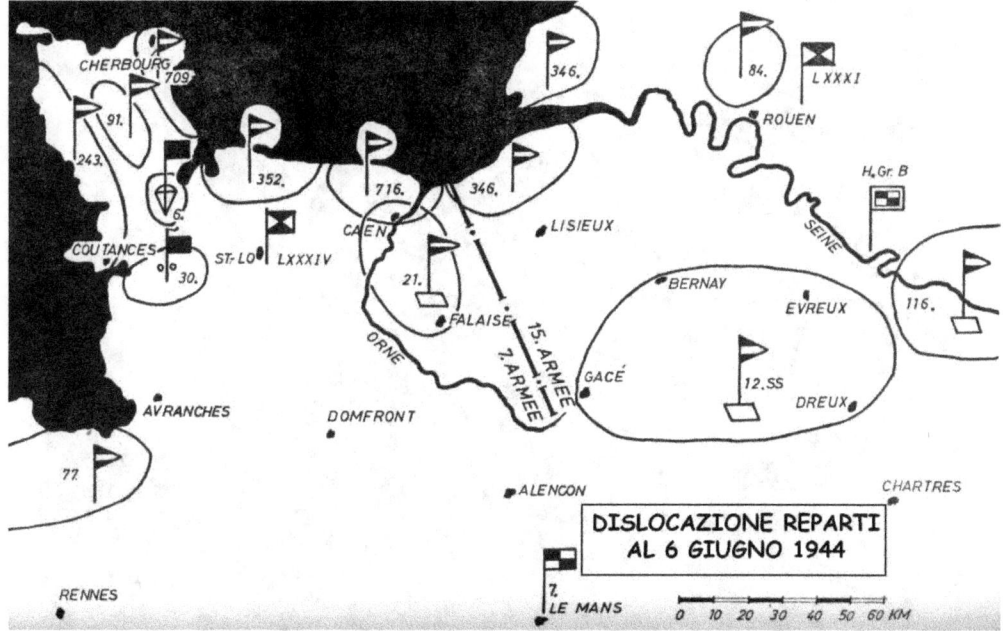

Deployment of German units in Normandy on 6 June 1944.

At around 04:00, all units of the division were ready for action: *SS-Pz.Gren.Rgt.25* began reconnaissance of the Caen area, while the division command communicated the alert status to the corps, without yet receiving any orders or information about what was happening. The troops of *716.* and *711.Infanterie-Division*, together with those of *21.Panzer-Division*, located near the bridges of Bénouville and east of the Orne River, began to attack the Allied paratroopers who had landed in the area. The landing of troops from the sea began around 06:30.

The Axis Forces

in World War Two 1939-1945

The intervention of the Hitlerjugend

Allied troops that have landed on the Normandy beaches, 6 June 1944. (US NARA)

At 4:45 am on June 6, 1944, the Supreme Command West (*Oberbefehlshaber West*) requested the intervention of the *Hitlerjugend* division, officially still in reserve, and of the 711 *Infanterie-Division* for possible use in the landing area. However, the official order did not come until 2.30 pm, that is about ten hours later, an inadmissible delay. In the meantime, following the launch of the Allied paratroopers in the sector of 711. *Inf.Div.*, headquarters of *15.Armee* requested that *Hitlerjugend* conduct a reconnaissance in the area: "... *the 12.SS-Panzer-Division, without neglecting its OKW reserve task, must immediately conduct reconnaissance in the area of 711. Infanterie-Division and observe the sector for a possible enemy landing from the air...* ".

A PzKpfw IV and Hitlerjugend motorcyclists on the march. (US NARA)

Ten minutes later, *Panzergruppe West* issued the march order to *Hitlerjugend*, the *711.Inf.Div.* and the *17.SS-Pz.Gren.Div. 'GvB'*. The headquarters of the *12.SS.Division* in turn passed the order down to its *Aufklärungs-Abteilung*.

tank! Pay particular attention along the way to possible ambushes by partisans, which have recently become more and more frequent. Marching sequence: a team of motorcycle riflemen, eight and four-wheeled armored cars, at a distance of about 50 meters, another team of motorcycle riflemen as a rear guard. Destination: the command post of the *Abteilung* '. *After about fifteen minutes we reached the command post and I reported to the commander, SS-Stubaf. Bremer. I received information on enemy air landings along the coastal area and behind our defensive positions, from the area west of the mouth of the Seine in Carentan ...*

A Hitlerjugend motorized column on the move. In the foreground is a Kubelwagen with the divisional insignia clearly visible on the right rear fender. In front of the motorcyclists is a SdKfz 250/1 and immediately in front of that is a Panther. (US NARA)

Our recon teams began their reconnaissance around 4:00 ... At 11:00, I sent a report: '... all along the coast, from Arromanches Bay to the west, passing through the mouth of the Orne River to the east, ships of all kinds are landing troops and firing at our coastal defenses. Tough fighting is taking place along the Courseulles-St. Aubin 'coastal road ".

American troops landing in Normandy.

A German vehicle on a Normandy road, completely covered with foliage, in an attempt to escape Allied air attacks. (US NARA)

More new orders

At 5:00 am, also on June 6, 15.*Armee* reported to the *Heeresgruppe* that Allied paratroopers were continuing to land in the Houlgate area. The availability of *Hitlerjugend* was therefore requested for its intervention in the area of the paratrooper landings. Half an hour later, the *Armee* requested that the division take action as soon as possible. However, *Generalleutnant* Speidel first wanted to discuss the situation with Supreme Command West. Ten minutes later, *Generalmajor* Pemsel, commander of 7.*Armee*, reported that the situation east of the Orne River was apparently calm, but that the enemy was still holding the bridge at Bénouville. Speidel after finally speaking with General Blumentritt, commander of Supreme Command West, learned that the *Heeresgruppe* had planned to deploy *Hitlerjugend* troops on both sides of Lisieux as soon as possible. Between 5:00 and 5:20, the Supreme Command West made the decision to assign the *Hitlerjugend* to *Heeresgruppe West*, without waiting for the approval of the OKH, then ordered the transfer of the division to the *711.Inf.Div.* sector, in order to be immediately engaged against the

The Axis Forces

German infantry and half-track units in Normandy.

A Somua S-35 engaged in Normandy.

SS-Oberführer Fritz Kramer in Normandy. (US NARA)

troops that had landed, in the Bernay – Lisieux - Vimoutiers area. The transfer order was sent from *Heeresgruppe* to *Panzergruppe West* at 5:50 am. The division was to make contact immediately with the general headquarters of the *LXXXI.Armee-Korps* in Rouen and with the *711.Inf.Div.* in Le Quesnay. At the same time the Flak companies of *SS-Pz.Gr.Rgt.26* were transferred back to the division, after having been engaged in the anti-aircraft defense of the Seine crossings at Elbeuf and Gaillon. Between 6:30 and 7:00, the transfer order arrived at the division headquarters, taking the staff by surprise: *Hitlerjugend* had in fact already deployed most of its advanced units, including the entire armored regiment, north of the Bernay-Lisieux line. According to the order received from the *Heeresgruppe*, the tanks would have to travel initially southwest and then north, northwest, in order to reach the sector of *711. Inf.Div.*, a useless and time-consuming march in terms of time and fuel. In addition, the division had already prepared a deployment plan on the ground, between the mouths of the Seine and Orne rivers, which thus had to be shelved.

Having to comply with the new provisions, the division found itself with its non-combatant service units forward and had to organize itself in an area of only 25 square kilometers!!! From this area there were only two viable roads towards the coast. The Lisieux crossing was particularly threatened by attacks from Allied fighter bombers. The division's chief of staff, *SS-Stubaf.* Hubert Meyer, telephoned his *I.SS-Panzer-Korps* counterpart, *SS-Brigdf.* Fritz Krämer, to try to have the orders revoked, but all his efforts were in vain, also taking into account that the division, despite being part of *I.SS-Panzer-Korps* together with the *LSSAH*, had been temporarily detached from it.

An SdKfz 251/10 towing a Pak 40 on the Normandy front, on the lookout for Allied air attacks.

A non-commissioned officer of the Hitlerjugend Division.

A new marching order for the new assembly area was then immediately prepared and passed on to the various unit commanders. The war diary of *I./SS-Pz.Gr.Rgt. 25* reported that the battalion received the alarm at 3:00 and the code word "*Blücher*" at 05:55. The unit was ready to move as early as 6:00. The code word "*Blücher*" indicated that the troops had to prepare to move to the designated departure points. The battalion began its march along the designated Plan Z road at 10:00, after receiving the order by radio from the regimental headquarters. The *Flak-Abteilung* received the departure order at 8:00 am together with the instructions for the anti-aircraft defense of the area around Lisieux. The second and fourth batteries, equipped with 88mm and 37mm pieces respectively, were supposed to cross the river at Les Andelys, but moved separately. The other units of the division were alerted between ten and eleven. The divisional command post initially remained in Acon as long as the telephone line worked, while another provisional headquarters was set up in Lisieux. The commander of *SS-Pz.Gr. Rgt. 25, SS-Staf.* Kurt Meyer, had started a reconnaissance action in the Caen area immediately after the alarm.

Panthers of *3./SS-Pz.Rgt.12* on the march. In the foreground is *SS-Ustuf.* Rolf Jauch.

A 20mm Flakvierling of an SS unit in Normandy.

During the day, the *Oberbefehlshaber West* became convinced that the landing of troops from the sea was limited to the strip of beach west of the mouth of the River Orne. In addition, *15.Armee* had reported to the *Heeresgruppe* at 10:20 am that a battalion of Allied paratroopers had been routed in the rear of *711.Inf.Div.* and that forty prisoners had been captured. Based on this optimistic information, *OOB West* ordered via *Panzergruppe West*, "... that *12.SS-Pz.Div.* had to prepare to move west ". The division certainly could not carry out that order given that the troops were already on their way to the new assembly area. At 2:32 pm, *OOB West* informed the *Heeresgruppe* that the OKW had transferred the *Hitlerjugend* to *7.Armee*.

However, it was still to be determined which headquarters the division should answer to. Soon thereafter, the *Heeresgruppe* was informed that the *Panzer-Lehr-Division* had also been 'liberated' from the OKW and that *OOB West* had advised them to move to the Flers area.

Hitlerjugend soldiers of the *SS-Pz.Aufkl.Abt.12*, spring 1944.

Kurt Meyer and Fritz Witt.

The *Hitlerjugend* and the *Pz-Lehr-Division* were then assigned to *7.Armee* to be engaged against the bridgehead in the sector of the *716. Inf.Div*. Army headquarters issued the following order through *Panzergruppe West*:

1) *12.SS-Pz-Div.* must be placed immediately north of the Alencon-Carrouges line on both sides of Evrecy, about eight kilometers southwest of Caen and is initially assigned to *LXXXIV.Armee-Korps*. Its mission is to intercept the enemy units that have just landed in the area west of the sector of the *21.Pz.Div.*, throw them back towards the sea and annihilate them.

2) *Pz-Lehr-Division* must instead be placed immediately south of the same line and initially must occupy the Flers-Vire area, about 50 kilometers south-west of Caen.

Soon after, it was decided to assign the *21.Pz.Div.*, the *12.SS-Pz.Div.*, the *Pz-Lehr-Division* and the *716.Inf.Div.* to *I.SS-Pz.Korps* and to transfer them to the right sector of *LXXXIV Armee-Korps*.

Transfer of units

The order from *Panzergruppe West* to move the division to the Caen area arrived at the *Hitlerjugend* command post at approximately 5:00 pm, when already part of the division had reached the new assembly areas. The *I./25*, led by *SS-Stubaf.* Hans Waldmüller, had reached St. Pierre-des-Ifs, six kilometers southwest of Lisieux, around 13:00, taking up positions on both sides of the road, with supplies and the rear of the battalion taking positions in Vimoutiers. With most of the troops on the march, no one at the divisional headquarters knew the situation in the Caen area: it was only known that the Allies had dropped paratroopers east of the River Orne and west of the mouth of the same river, so they had to conduct reconnaissance in the new assembly area and from there to the coast. Arrangements for regiments and battalions along the way required that, in the new grouping area, *SS-Pz.Gr.Rgt.26* commanded by *SS-Ostubaf.* Monhke together with the *I.Pz.Abteilung*, under the leadership of *SS-Stubaf.* Jürgensen, were to take position on the right flank of the area, while *SS-Pz.Gr.Rgt.26* of *SS-Staf.* Kurt Meyer with *II.Pz.Abteilung* led by *SS-Stubaf.* Prinz was on the left flank. The divisional commander, *SS-Brigdf.* Witt, together with his staff, went to St. Pierre-sur-Dives to the command post of *21.Pz.Div.*, to learn about the situation on the ground. The divisional staff operations group together with an escort company left Acon at 18:00 to move to Les Moutiers-en-Cinglais, 17 kilometers southwest of Caen, on the southern side of the Grimbosq Forest. The division's chief of staff, Hubert Meyer, arrived at the new *Hitlerjugend* command post in Les Moutiers during the night. During the afternoon, the OKW had ordered all units to quickly make all moves taking advantage of bad weather conditions. For his part, the commander of *Panzergruppe West*, General Geyr von Schweppenburg, advised regrouping the panzer divisions only after 20:00, to avoid Allied air attacks. The march of the *Hitlerjugend* units, especially from the early afternoon, had been greatly hampered by the attacks of Allied fighter bombers. The columns were forced to stop and continually seek

SS-Stubaf. Hans Waldmüller.

SS-Stubaf. Karl-Heinz Prinz.

shelter. After each attack, the destroyed or damaged vehicles had to be removed immediately from the road, the wounded and dead were instead left to the personnel of the rearguard services.

Half-tracks resume their march after an air attack.

Awesome photo of a rocket fired from a Typhoon fighter against a German convoy on the road.

A self-propelled gun in Normandy, June 1944.

Testimony of *Sturmmann* Martin Besel, member of *I. Zug* of the *13.Kompanie* of *SS-Pz.Gr.Rgt.25*: *"... During our march we were attacked by enemy fighter bombers. Our commander 'Panzermeyer' was particularly lucky on that occasion, jumping out of his vehicle just in time. He threw himself down on the left, while a bomb exploded on the right side, completely destroying his vehicle. The attack was aimed at a bridge which, thank God, remained intact."* Initially it was felt that the attacks by Allied aviation had resulted in heavy losses, but in reality, this was not the case. For example, the divisional escort company reported no casualties and no injuries during its June 6 march.

Area of operations

Hitlerjugend grenadiers.

In any case, the Allied air strikes slowed the march of the division's units and therefore only a part of them reached the area southwest of Caen on 6 June. The *I./25* arrived at Missy, 15 kilometers southwest of Caen, on the Caen-Villers Bocage road, at the end of the day. The unit led by *SS-Stubaf.* Hans Waldmüller initially camped in a forest southeast of the village, then marched on foot to take up position along the railway line northwest of Noyers, about a mile northwest of Missy, around 23:00. A reconnaissance group, led by *SS-Ustuf.* Paul Exner, advanced towards Tilly-sur-Seulles, eight kilometers northwest of Missy. The other two battalions of *SS-Pz.Gr.Rgt.25*, the divisional staff and the regimental support companies, reached their grouping area at about the same time. *II.Panzer Abteilung* and *III.Artillerie Abteilung* arrived in the area southwest of Caen during the night between 6 and 7 June.

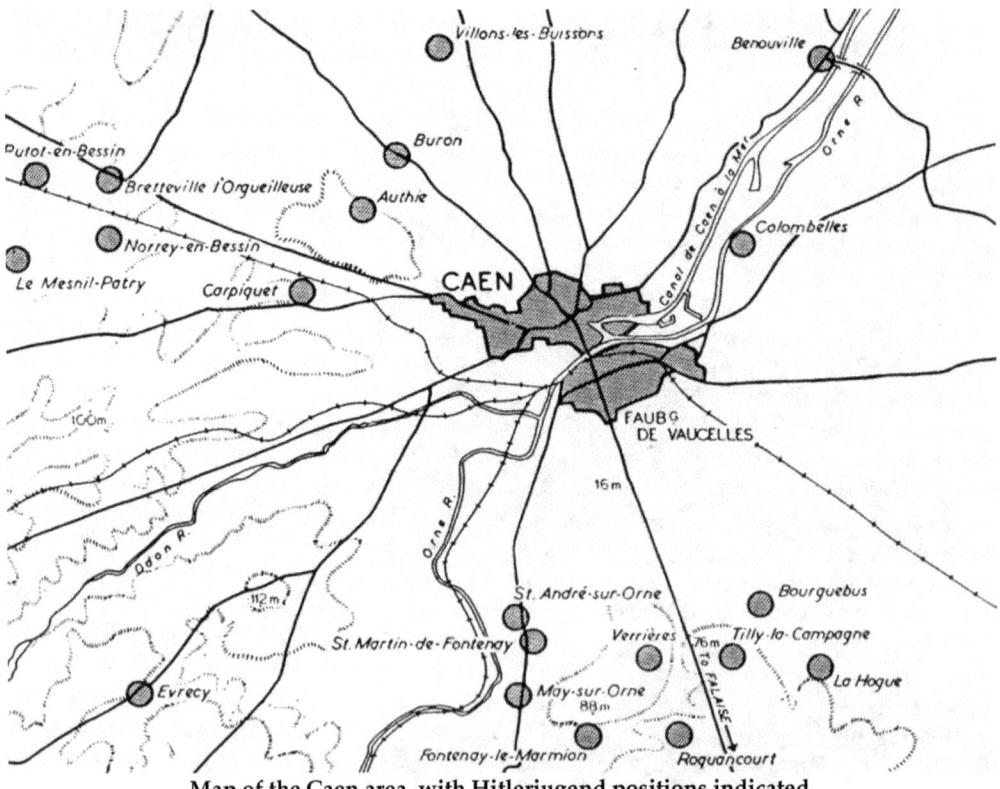
Map of the Caen area, with **Hitlerjugend** positions indicated.

The batteries marched together with the battalions with which they were to operate: the *7.Batterie* with the *I./25*, the *8.Batterie* with the *II./25*, the *9.Batterie* with the *III./25* and so on. *SS-Pz.Gr.Rgt. 26*, the *I. Panzer Abteilung*, the *Pionier-Bataillon*, the *I. Artillerie-Abteilung*, the

The Axis Forces

Kurt Meyer. (US NARA)

II.Artillerie-Abteilung and the *Flak Abteilung*, took up positions in the Lisieux area. Of course, all the delays recorded by the units were the direct consequence of the contradictory orders of the German High Command.

The battle for Caen begins

SS-Staf. Kurt Meyer had travelled at the head of his regiment to reach the command post of the *716. Infanterie-Division*, located in a bunker in the Folie area. He arrived around midnight on 6 June and met with *Generalleutnant* Richter and the commander of *21.Pz.Div.*, *Generalmajor* Feuchtinger. The situation appeared critical: *716.Inf.Div.* had been defeated and the road to Caen was open to the Allied forces. Furthermore, Feuchtinger did not have a clear view of the situation and of the positions of the various *Kampfgruppen* in his division. The commander of the *21.Pz.Div.*himself reported to Meyer that there was the possibility that the city and the airfield at Carpiquet, were already in the hands of the Allies. *SS-Staf.* Meyer then immediately ordered a reconnaissance of the entire area to be sure of this: after about an hour, it was ascertained that Carpiquet, Rots and Buron were free from the enemy. Scattered elements of *716. Inf.Div.* had been sighted in Buron, while the position of Les Buissons had been captured.

Elements of the 12.SS after an air attack on one of their columns.

As soon as Meyer left the bunker to return to his command post, housed in a small café in Saint Germain la Blanche west of the Caen exit, he received a call from *SS-Brigdf.* Witt, present at that time near the command post of the *21.Pz.Div.* in St. Pierre-sur-Dives. Witt informed Meyer about the *I.SS-Pz.Korp* order, which stipulated that *21.Pz.Div.* should attack to the left of the front, at 16:00 on 7 June, to throw the enemy back into the sea.

The PzKpfw.IV '536' of *SS-Uscha*. Willy Kretzchmar advances to action, June 1944.

Hitlerjugend grenadiers, June 1944.

The day before, *21.Pz.Div.* had attacked on the left of the Orne River with only two *Kampfgruppen*, while another *Kampfgruppe* was engaged against the Allied paratroopers to the right of the same river. A large breach was present on the right flank of the *Hitlerjugend* concentration area, in the Verson-Rots sector. *SS-Brigdf.* Witt then ordered *SS-Staf.* Meyer to attack in the sector to the right of *SS-Pz.Gr.Rgt.26* and to do this, he had to move from his assembly area on the left flank, to establish contact with the left flank of *21.Panzer-Division*. Furthermore, as a precondition for the concentration of the units, Witt ordered that the area around the Carpiquet airport should be protected under all circumstances. The attack by *SS-Pz.Gr.Rgt.25* was to be supported by *III.Artillerie-Abteilung*, which had marched together with the regiment, and by the other artillerymen of

II.Pz.Abteilung that arrived with them. The crest of Mue was designated as the dividing line between the two *Panzergrenadier* regiments of the division.

A Hitlerjugend *sIG 33* on the Normandy Front, June 1944 (Michael Cremin Collection).

Hitlerjugend grenadiers, June 1944.

Orders for the attack

At around 3:00, *SS-Staf.* Meyer verbally issued the order for his regiment to attack, according to which two battalions of armored grenadiers were to attack in line, the *I.Bataillon* on the right and the *II.Bataillon* on the left, with *III.Bataillon* in reserve. To do this, *I. Bataillon* had to regroup on the left flank of *21.Pz.Div.* between Epron and La Folie, *II.Bataillon* in Bitot and *III.Bataillon* southeast of Franqueville south of the Caen-Bayeux road. A platoon of heavy infantry guns (*13./25*) and a platoon of light *Flak* pieces (*14./25*) were assigned to each battalion, while the bulk of *16.Kompanie* (pioneers) was attached to *I./25*. The *III.Artillerie-Abteilung* had to take a position so as to be able to provide support fire on the entire attack front of the regiment, while a battery of heavy guns was to cooperate with each of the battalions. The *Panzer-Regiment* was ordered to support the attack on a wide front, with the men of *II.Abteilung* arriving, as also the *15.(Aufklärungs) Kompanie* was to cover the left flank of the attack front. Meyer's command post was placed in Ardenne Abbey, while the division moved its command to the southwestern exit of Caen, in the Venoix district, along the Caen-Villers Bocage road. The SS grenadiers marched all night to reach their grouping area.

Artillery observers in the bell tower of the Abbey of Ardenne. (US NARA)

A *PzKpfw.IV* covered in foliage, ready to attack.

SS-Staf. Meyer observed these movements from his command post: "... *the commander of I. Bataillon came to report. I was quickly briefed on the situation, we knew that a difficult confrontation was ahead of us. The men of the battalion had jumped from the vehicles and trucks, disappearing into the darkness. No vehicle crossed the city, everyone headed south ... The grenadiers were approaching. Very calmly, without letting emotions show but with the firm determination to be ready for their baptism of fire ...* ".

III./SS-Artillerie-Abteilung 12 also established its command post in the Ardenne Abbey, from whose towers it was possible to observe the entire attack sector of the regiment and also that of *21.Pz.Div.. SS-Staf.* Meyer drove to his forward command post in the Abbey around 9:00 am, aboard a Kubelwagen after avoiding the Allied fighter bombers that infested the area. In one of the towers of the Abbey, *SS-Stubaf.* Bartling [2], commander of *III.Artillerie-Abteilung*, told him that he was ready to open fire. At the same time, the three grenadier battalions reported that they had reached their positions for the attack, while *II./Pz.Abt.12* was yet to arrive.

Preparation for the attack of 7 June, in the courtyard of the Abbey of Ardenne. From left, *SS-Stubaf.* Erick Urbanitz, commander of *I.(gep)/SS-Pz.Art.Rgt. 12*, *SS-Stubaf.* Karl-Heinz Prinz, commander of *II./SS-Pz.Rgt.12* and *SS-Stubaf.* Karl Bartling, commander of *II./SS-Pz.art.Rgt.12*.

SS-Uscha. Klempt on his *PzKpfw.IV*.

From his position, Meyer spotted *II.Bataillon*, as his recon patrols disappeared in the direction of the enemy. Only around 10:00, the first panzers appeared and shortly after, *SS-Stubaf.* Prinz reported that about fifty tanks were ready for action. The others would arrive later in the day and the next night.

The panzers reached their attack positions: *8.Pz.Kp.* with five panzers in the *I.Bataillon* sector, *7.Pz.Kp.* and *6.Pz.Kp.* to the right and left of the Abbey, *5.Pz.Kp.* southeast of Franqueville positioned behind a slope south of the Caen-Bayeux road with *III.Bataillon* and the *9.Pz.Kp.* in reserve, behind *5.Pz.Kp.*

The Axis Forces

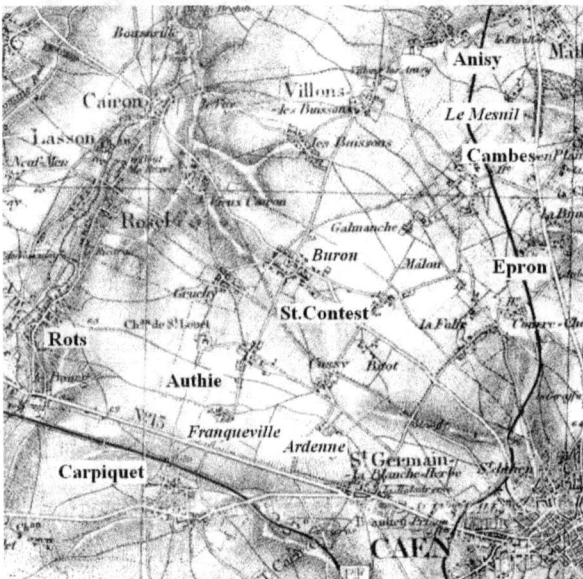
A *PzKpfw.IV* covered in foliage, ready to attack.

Map of the area where the fighting took place.

Hitlerjugend's grenadier near a destroyed Sherman.

The enemy situation

Meanwhile, the Allies were also preparing for the attack on Caen, in particular the British 3rd Infantry Division, ready to attack the sector assigned to *21.Pz.Div.*, whose right flank bordered the *Hitlerjugend* sector. The 2nd Battalion of the Royal Ulster Rifles, reinforced by a tank company from the East Riding Yeomanry, was advancing behind the positions of the 1st Battalion of the King's Own Scottish Borderers at Le Mesnil, just in the direction of the attack front of *I./SS -Pz.Gr.Rgt.25*. The vanguard of the 9th Canadian Infantry Brigade, the Nova Scotia Highlanders, regrouped on the morning of June 7, with the aim of reaching Carpiquet airfield. This included the North Nova Scotia Highlanders and the 27th Armored Regiment (The Sherbrooke Fusiliers Regiment). The Stuart tanks of the armored reconnaissance units advanced first, followed by a company of the Highlanders, loaded onto the Bren carriers. Immediately behind was a platoon of machine guns, a platoon of anti-tank guns, two groups of pioneers and four other anti-tank guns. The bulk of the brigade, including three other infantry companies, followed soon after, with men loaded onto Sherman tanks.

Near Villons-les-Buissons, the vanguard came under fire from some Flak pieces and some Paks, but after a pincer attack, the position was cleared. Around 12 noon, the village of Buron, defended by isolated elements of *716. Inf.Div.*, was

in World War Two 1939-1945

also conquered, after which the march continued in the direction of Authie. *SS-Staf.* Meyer had been scanning the battlefield with his binoculars since morning: he had received the news that a large Allied armored formation was gathering in the area south of Colomby-sur-Thaon. Shortly after, he was able to identify that the Allied tanks were arriving behind the *II./25* from Buron in the direction of Authie. He then gave the order to wait until the enemy was in range before opening fire and above all to wait for his order. At the same time, *SS-Ustuf.* Porsch[(3)], went on a patrol with his four PzKpfw IVs of *5.Pz.Kp.*, along the Franqueville-Authie road. At around 2:00 pm, he unexpectedly ran into the Sherbrooke Fusiliers' Shermans from Authie. In the brief firefight that followed, three of his panzers were lost: those of *SS-Hscha.* Müller, of SS-*Oscha.* Auinger and *SS-Uscha.* Klempt.

SS-Ostubaf. Karl-Heinz Milius, left, in conversation with a soldier.

PzKpfw.IV '536' firing against allied tanks, June 1944.

Upon receiving the news, Meyer immediately ordered the commander of *SS-Pz.Rgt.12*, *SS-Ostubaf.* Max Wünsche, who was there with him, to join the armored companies located on the left flank and to the commander of the *III./25*, *SS-Ostubaf.* Karl-Heinz Milius, to join the panzer attack with his battalion. Returning to his tanks, Wünsche transmitted the order to attack his unit commanders: "..*Achtung, Panzer Marsch!*".

The Axis Forces

PzKpfw.IV of *SS-Uscha*. Willy Kretzchmar.

PzKpfw.IV '626' engaged in combat.

Then, via radio, he transmitted the order to *II.Pz.Abt.* to regroup its companies on the left. The *6.Pz.Kp.*, located to the left of the Abbey and the *5.Pz.Kp.*, immediately attacked without waiting a moment. Attacked on the flank, the Allied tanks were completely taken by surprise and within minutes several Shermans were knocked out. *6.Pz.Kp.* destroyed more than ten Allied tanks, but suffered the loss of five PzKpfw IVs. After this first firefight, the panzers continued in the direction of Authie, followed by the *Panzergrenadieren* of *9.Kompanie*, who marched on foot. Authie was conquered shortly thereafter. The panzers of *6.Pz.Kp.* went around the city and continued in the direction of Buron.

SS-Sturmmann Hans Fenn, gunner in the *I. Zug* of the *6.Pz.Kp.*, wrote about this battle: *"... Ostuf. Gasch, came to us, taking command of the point platoon, the I .Zug. We delivered some prisoners to the grenadiers without getting off our panzers, then continued to advance, only to find ourselves shortly after in a flat open area under fire from Canadian anti-tank guns. Four of my platoon tanks were destroyed. We, in the fifth tank, were hit by a direct hit between the side and the turret as we attempted to escape the fire of the enemy anti-tank guns. We were unable to hit Canadian fire positions at a distance of 1,500, 2,000 meters. A shell passed through the legs of my commander, Oscha. Esser, but he managed to get out of the turret. Since it was a phosphorus grenade, the whole tank caught fire. Somehow, I managed to get out of the tank through the loader's hatch, falling on the ground half burned, I went back to our grenadiers who followed behind. Our medical NCO took me to the field hospital in a car. "*

Testimony of *SS-Sturmmann* Karl Vasold of *9./SS-Pz.Gr.Rgt.25*, on the same attack: *"... The order came, we march! We had to attack in the direction of Authie with the support of the panzers. We were soon under enemy fire and suffered our first losses. Some Canadian tanks on the outskirts of the city were destroyed, then house-to-house fighting followed after which the city was conquered. Our next target was the castle of St. Louis west of Authie. Here we suffered an intense defensive fire from some Canadian anti-tank guns. Some of our panzers were hit. The survivors of the burning crews were transferred to the rear ... We gathered on the outskirts of the city to take stock of the situation ... ".* **(To be continued).**

Bibliography
Massimiliano Afiero, "*12th SS Panzer Division Hitlerjugend: From Formation to the Battle of Caen*", Casemate Pub & Book Dist Llc

Italian light tanks CV L3/33-35-38
by Luca Cristini

Introduction

Created in the early 1930s to supply the Italian army with a large-scale light tank, the L3 remained at the forefront of armoured units until 1941. Although it only played an important role in the fighting of the Ethiopian campaign and the Spanish Civil War, the 'sardine box' was later limited to anti-partisan combat and support of occupation troops after the difficult start of the Second World War. Due to its characteristics, the L33 or CV33 light tank was better known to Italian soldiers as the 'sardine box', 'steel coffin' or 'death box'; not very reassuring names given by Italian tank drivers to what was intended, in the intentions of the Italian high command at the start of the Second World War, to be an assault tank. Even the term 'light tank' today appears to be an understatement (even the Sherman was considered a light tank, and weighed a good 30 tonnes compared to just over 3 of the early L3s). The fast tank was certainly the most famous and well-known among Italian tanks of all time. In spite of its meagre war capabilities, it was widely used on all war fronts where the Royal Italian Army was engaged. Produced in large numbers considering the country's industrial capacity in the 1930s, around 2,000 examples were built from 1933 until 1938, when production ceased.

This photo of an L 3/35 from the 32nd Rgt. of the Ariete Division in North Africa gives a good idea of the size of the Italian light tank.

Wooden model presented by Ansaldo in 1929. It is very far from the prototype's forms.

The development

In 1928, General Cavallero, then Undersecretary of War, decided to equip the Regio Esercito with a light reconnaissance tank to accompany the infantry. The British *Carden-Loyd Mk.VI* tankette caught the attention of the Technical Automotive Inspectorate, which decided to test it in Italy. As the results were not entirely satisfactory, the Ansaldo company was commissioned to develop a more suitable variant in line with the Italian army's expectations. Ansaldo began by building a wooden model that was presented in 1929. The prototype light tank, very different from the model, was built in 1930 by engineer Rosini. Its rolling train was inspired by the Carden-Loyd, but it had three pairs of wheels on each side instead of two. However, the body and superstructure were enlarged to accommodate a more powerful engine and to improve habitability. The vehicle was intended to tow a two-axle tracked trailer.

The 1930 prototype pulling a crawler trailer.

The prototype of the armored transport on the left, and that of the light tank on the right.

As the chassis suspension was unsatisfactory, Ansaldo modified the undercarriage of the prototype in 1931; a guide roller was added in front of the tensioning wheel. A second prototype was also built for battlefield supply, without a roof and with a redesigned cogwheel. This armoured transport prototype was tested at the same time as the standard wagon and served as the basis for further developments. After testing near Genoa, a pre-series of four was ordered in 1932. On these vehicles, the original water-cooled Fiat mod.14 6.5 mm machine gun was replaced by an air-cooled Fiat mod.14 aviation gun. Front mudguards were also added, two headlights and the side grilles were moved to the sides of the cockpit.

Technical characteristics

The tank consisted of the chassis (or hull), the armament, the engine and its transmission, locomotion and control components. The vehicle had a mass of 3.2 tonnes. It was 3.17 metres long, 1.4 metres wide and 1.3 metres high.

The hull: it consisted of steel plates rigidly connected so as to form a non-deformable complex. The armour plating ranged from a minimum of 6 to 14 mm and provided sufficient protection from bullets fired from rifles and machine guns, shrapnel or minor artillery hits. It consisted of two side walls, a front, a rear and an upper wall, a bottom and a turret. Two bulkheads divided the inside of the hull into three chambers. Starting from the first at the front of the craft, we have: the combat chamber, the engine chamber, and finally, at the rear, the one for the cooling organs. In the first one we find: the crew, composed of two people (tank leader on the left and pilot on the right), the armament, the transmission and control organs and the fuel tank, in the second, the engine and, in the third, the radiator. The turret includes several plates: in one of the front plates there is a casemate housing for the weapons and in another there is an opening, closed by a flap, for the pilot's forward view; the upper one has two openings - for the entry and exit of the two crew members - that can be closed with flaps; in the rear one there are also two openings, with flaps, for the rear view. Slits for the side view were also added on the later versions.

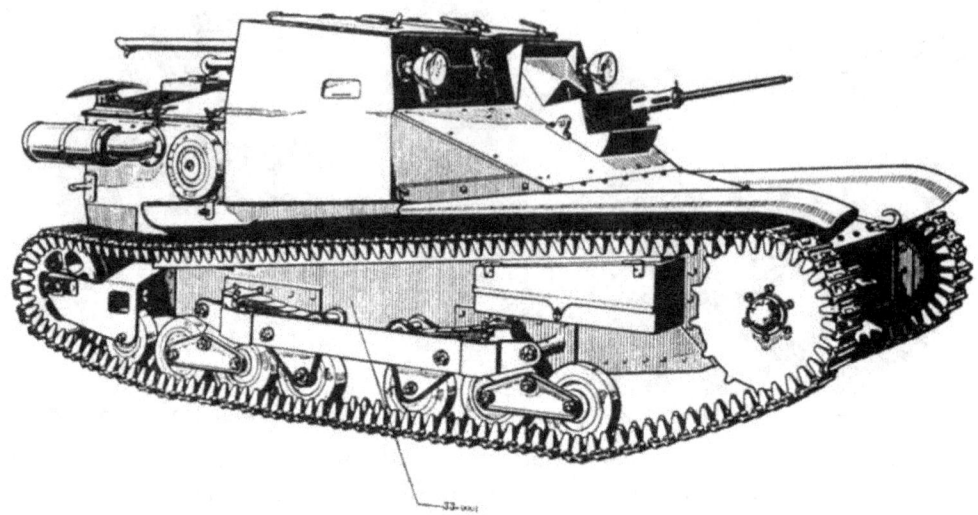

Drawing of the CV 33 series 1. Note the toolbox latch, the shuttle on the side of the cab, and the common support for the guide roller and tension wheel.

Armament: the most common weaponry consisted of two paired Fiat cal. 8 machine guns, or a Fiat cal. 8 machine gun, or a flamethrower: all were housed in a mobile casemate, by means of a cradle and retaining pin. They were loaded and manoeuvred from inside the cockpit by the wagon master. The installation provided the weapons with a horizontal firing sector of 40° (20° to the right and 20° to the left); a firing range of 20° in depression and 20° in elevation, relative to the horizontal carriage. Other types of armament were tested and loaded such as the Swiss Solothurn heavy machine gun and others.

Engine: it was mounted transversely at the rear. It consisted of four vertical, single-block, fourstroke cylinders and developed a power of 43 HP at normal speed, energy was transmitted to two drive wheels. It was started by hand, by means of a crank, either from outside or inside the tank. The engine guaranteed a maximum speed of 42 km/h with an operating range of about 125 km.

Transmission organs: consisting of the drive shaft, clutch, gearbox and steering mechanism. The propeller shaft connects the engine shaft with the clutch and transmits motion to the gearbox and then to the steering mechanism. The gearbox can provide four speeds for forward and one for reverse and, through the reduction gear, a second set of reduced speeds (four for forward and one for reverse).

Locomotive parts: consisting of drive wheels, idlers, track chains, track support beam, auxiliary rollers, bogies with load-bearing rollers. The driving wheels, made of steel, are located at the front of the wagon, one on each side. Each wheel consists of a toothed disc

(15 teeth) on which the tracks engage. The deflection wheels are made of bronze, located at the rear of the wagon (one on each side); they turn in neutral on a pin and they are connected to the auxiliary rollers. The action of a sleeve makes it possible to vary the position of the pin of the idler wheel and thus increase or decrease the tension of the track.

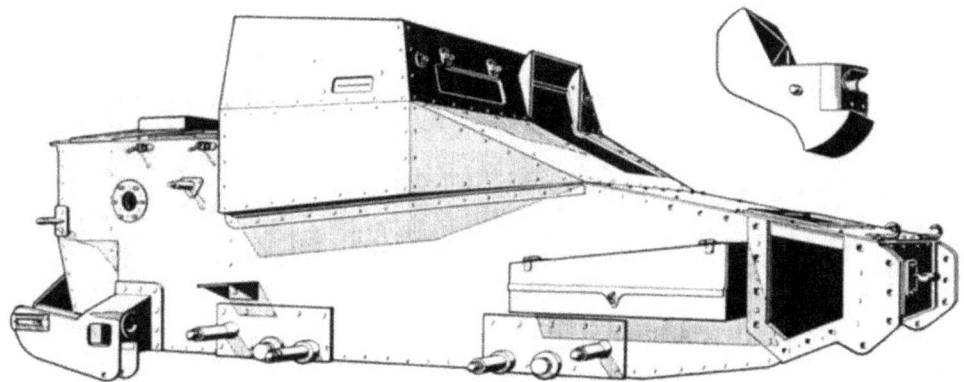

Drawing of CV 33 series 1 body, made of metal sheet assembled by riveting and brazing.

The tracks, two in number, one on each side, are composed of 72 main and 72 auxiliary links, of pressed steel, connected by pins and plates. Each main link has a window –into which the drive wheel teeth penetrate– and two fins that serve to guide the load-bearing rollers and prevent slipping. Each main link also has two ribs for gripping the track to the ground and, on the side, three perforated appendages for the passage of the connecting pin. The auxiliary links are devoid of the outer ribs and window.

CV 3-05, 4-cylinder in-line gasoline engine.

The acacia-wood, trapezoidal-section track-bearing spars, designed to support the track above, are also two and arranged on the sides of the tank. The load-bearing bogies constitute, together with leaf springs, the suspension of the wagon and there are two per side, connected by spars rigidly attached to the sides of the wagon. Each bogie is equipped with three rubberised, load-bearing rollers. The bogies distribute the weight of the tank sufficiently evenly over the load-bearing rollers; they also allow elastic suspension of the hull and enable the track to adapt to uneven terrain.

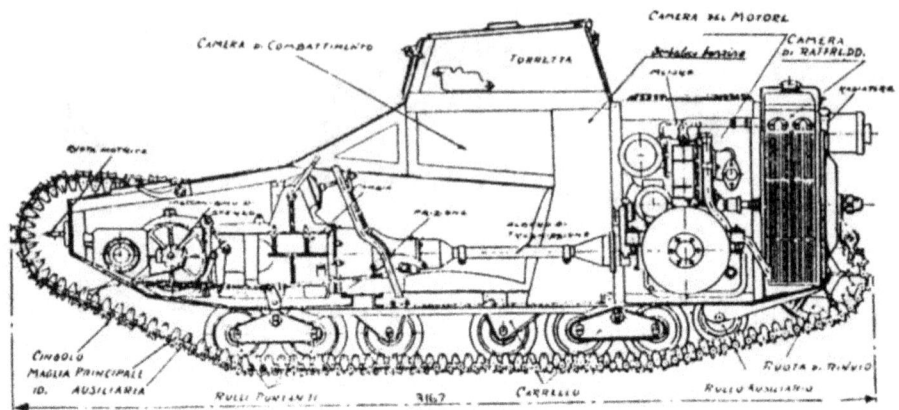

Drawing from the original manual of the Longitudinal Section of a CV 33 Series 1.

Control elements: these are operated by two control or direction levers. Located inside the hull, to the right and left of the driver, they each control two steering mechanism locking blocks; a brake pedal intensifies the block locking action and a clutch pedal and levers control the clutch. The levers, pedals and shackles, acting under the action of the driver, allow straight travel, right and left rotation and stopping of the wagon. The rotation of the wagon is obtained by slowing down or stopping the motion of one of the tracks through the action of the control or direction levers (the tank rotates on the side from which the braking or locking of the track has occurred); stopping is obtained following the simultaneous locking of the two, tracks.

Fossati factory, Genoa - Sestri Ponente, light tank production sector.

Vehicle Versions

Numerous versions of the light fast tank were produced, including definitive operatives and prototypes, the most important of which are listed below.

- *CV33 1st Series*: first designation of Ansaldo's fast tank, armed with a Fiat 14 cal. 6.5 mm aviation machine gun. All 1st Series tanks were later rearmed by a gun of the same type, adapted to 8 mm calibre.

- *CV33 2nd Series (Mod.34)*: appearing in 1934 but distributed in 1936, this version introduced the twin 8 mm FIAT Mod.14 machine gun and the separation of the tensioning wheel from the rear wheel. The hinges of the pilot hatch are inside the body, the replacement of the rear doors with hatches, the ventilation door protected by a metal plate and other changes to the external fittings complete the version. In 1938, these copies were renamed L3 / 33 then L33 in 1940.

CV 33 tanks in training before the war. (P. Crippa Archives)

- *CV35 1st Series*: variant of the previous series. The differences are reduced to a few welded rather than riveted body plates. The initial guns were replaced by FIAT Mod.35 or Breda Mod.38 machine guns. In 1938, this series was renamed L3 /35 then L35 in 1940.

- *CV35 2nd Series*: almost the same as the previous one, with minor modifications in terms of details and embrasures.

- *CV30 or L3/38*: this series was tested in 1937. The prototype had a new gear, with an enlarged diameter for the four bogie wheels and a new suspension. The two 8 mm machine guns were replaced by Breda Mod.31 Type Marina 13.2 mm models. From 1940 this model was called the L38.

• *L3 lf (C.V. Flamethrower)*: its development began in 1935. It mounted a flame thrower tube in the place of one of the machine guns, which was fed by an external tank that could be either mounted on the engine inspection hatch or on a special trailer. The modification was carried out on both C.V.33 and C.V.35 hulls. The vehicle therefore weighed 5 tonnes. This vehicle was used in Abyssinia, Spain, France, the Balkans, North Africa and Italian East Africa.

• *L3/r (C.V. With radio equipment)*: equipped with a radio and used as a command tank, intended for squadron (or company) or squadron group (or battalion) commanders.

• *L3 (Fast gangway tank)*: adapted for the transport and deployment of a gangway with a maximum length of 6/7 metres. Without armament. Prototype.

• *L3 (Recovery fast tank)*: equipped at the rear with a coupling system for recovering damaged or broken-down tanks. Prototype.

• *L3 (Solothurn fast tank)*: modification carried out on only a few examples directly at operational units in North Africa in 1941. Instead of twin machine guns it was equipped with a Swiss Solothurn S-18/1000 20 mm anti-tank gun.

• *L35 Airborne*: flamethrower version of the L3/35, suitable for airborne transport.

• *CV33 Training*: from 1941 some units, withdrawn from the front line as obsolete, and deprived of armament were used for tank training.

• *Trubia*: experimental version designed for nationalist Spain, armed with a 20 mm Breda Mod.35 cannon.

• *L3 light tractor*: version designed as a light tractor for a 47/32 mm cannon.

• *L3 demolition tractor*: a unique radio-controlled prototype intended for the destruction of minefields or fortifications, an idea similar to the German Goliath.

• *L3 47/32 self-propelled gun*: only two prototypes of this open-hulled self-propelled gun were made, one by Fiat and the other by Breda. Vehicle equipped with a 47 mm anti-tank gun.

The weapons enciclopædia
ITALIAN LIGHT TANKS
CV L3/33-35-38

SERIES EDITED BY Luca Cristini Editore (Soldiershop), via Orio, 35/4 - 24050 Zanica (BG) ITALY.

The Totenkopf Division on the Eastern Front October 1943 – January 1944
by Massimiliano Afiero

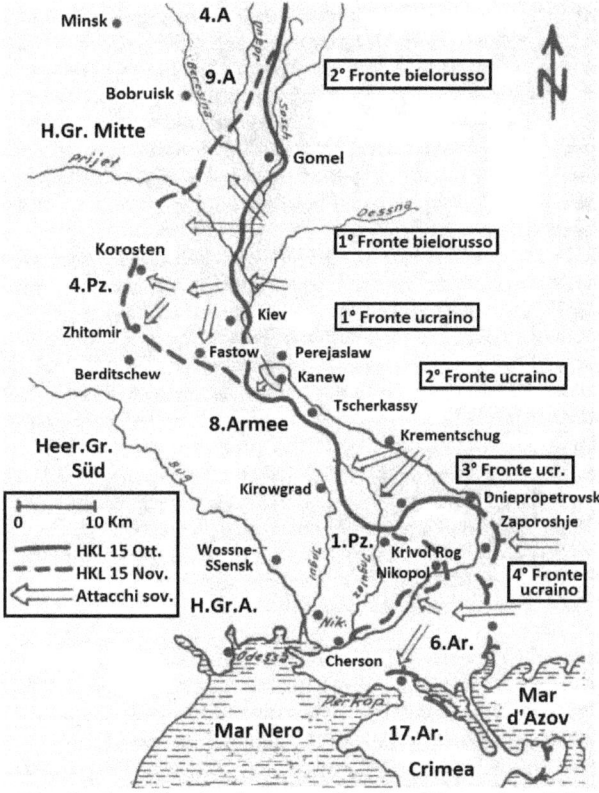

The Soviet offensive between October-November 1943.

A German defensive position in the Reschetilowka sector.

At the beginning of October 1943, the *Totenkopf* was deployed along the western bank of the Dnieper, in the area southwest of Kremenchuk, between Kutschanowka and Uspenskoje. The SS troops had no time to rest, because there was no defensive line along the river and they had to construct new positions in haste. At the same time, they had to provide troops to support the attack of the *106.Inf.Division* against the bridgehead that the Soviets had established west of Koleberda. The division headquarters was also busy reorganizing several units; accordingly, the anti-tank group and the assault gun group were merged temporarily, under the command of *SS-Stubaf.* Grünert. On October 15, 1943, the 2nd Ukrainian Front attacked the left flank of *1.Panzerarmee* with the objective of capturing Krivoy-Rog, a vital communications hub for the German army. Its loss would have led to the isolation and destruction of German forces engaged at the mouth of the Dnieper and the Nikopol bridgehead. The Soviets made a deep penetration to the east of Annowka, in the *XI.Armee-Korps* rear area. On October 16, von Manstein ordered *8.Armee* to commit the *Totenkopf* against the flanks of the Soviet penetration. The division's troops accordingly assembled during the night between the 17th and 18th in the Pawlysch-Onufrijewka sector. Shortly after, however, von Manstein himself decided to postpone the attack in order to wait for the arrival of fresh reinforcements with which he could more effectively hit the flanks of the Soviet offensive. On October 19, the enemy forces attacked the positions at Pjatichatki.

Totenkopf soldiers during a lull in combat, Autumn 1943.

A *Totenkopf* MG-34 machine gun team.

Several train convoys full of damaged tanks and various material, as well as two hospital trains loaded with wounded soldiers from the *Totenkopf* and *8.SS-Kavallerie-Division*, were standing at the station. A counterattack mounted by *I./Pz.Rgt.15* recaptured the area around the station; however, when the tankers examined the two trainloads of wounded soldiers, they found only two survivors because everyone else, including the medical personnel, had been massacred by the Soviets. Around 10:00 the Soviets got behind the positions at Selenoje, where *SS-Feldersatz-Bataillon 3* and *SS-Genesenden-Abt.3* were located. The division's depot battalion was formed of young recruits from the classes of 1925 and 1926 who had never fought before. Towards evening, these young recruits took up positions east of Selenoje with orders to hold as long as possible, in order to allow the convalescent battalion to be evacuated.

The Soviets unleashed their attack, and despite having destroyed five T-34 tanks at close range, *SS-Feldersatz-Bataillon 3* was almost completely wiped out. Meanwhile, the rest of the division regrouped between Losowatka, Skybkoje and Iwanowka, subordinated to *XL.Pz.Korps*. The situation continued to grow increasingly critical and the threat against Krivoy-Rog intensified. On October 20, the *Totenkopf* prepared to counterattack.

Totenkopf motorcycle scouts on the move, Autumn 1943 (NARA).

Panzers and SS grenadiers, 1943.

SS-Pz.Rgt.3, with four *Bef.Pz.*, two *PzKpfw III*, eight *PzKpfw IV* and six *PzKpfw VI Tiger*, was kept in reserve at Iwanowka. The tanks and *SPW* of *6.Pz.Div.* were subordinated to the division.

3.SS-Pz.Division "Totenkopf"

On October 22, *11.Panzer-Division*, reinforced by *gep.Gruppe "Biermeier"*, attacked from Nawo Starodup. The Soviets were overrun and forced to withdraw to the northeast. That same day the division was officially re-baptized as the *3.SS-Panzerdivision "Totenkopf"*. *SS-Pz.Gren.Rgt.1 "Totenkopf"* was renumbered and became the *SS-Pz.Gren.Rgt.5 "Thule"*. *SS-Pz.Gren.Rgt.3 "Theodor Eicke"* became *SS-Pz.Gren.Rgt.6 "Theodor Eicke"*. All other divisional units were assigned the identification number "3", along with the prefix "Panzer-". On October 24, *XL.Pz.Korps*, reinforced by the *14.Pz.Div.* and *24.Pz.Div.*, was transferred to *8.Armee* in an attempt to destroy the Soviet forces that were located to the west of Ingulez. The following day the German command specified that the attack was to be launched along a north-south axis from the Kukulowka-Tscherwona-Kamenka area towards Sheltoje and Selenoje. Preparations were accelerated because the Soviets were already at the gates of Krivoy-Rog. On October 27, on orders of *1.Panzerarmee*, the division received as reinforcements the *He.StugG-Abt.278*, with twenty-one assault guns.

An 88 mm *Flak* gun of *SS-Flak-Abteilung 'Totenkopf'*, Autumn 1943 (NARA).

A *Totenkopf* soldier in a foxhole.

In addition, twelve panzers arrived from *Das Reich*. In the evening, *SS-Pz.Rgt.3* reported the status of its operational vehicles: four *Bef.Pz.*, two *PzKpfw III*, two *PzKpfw IV* and five *PzKpfw VI Tiger* tanks.

The next day, *XL.Pz.Korps* finally began its attack against the 1st and 5th Guards Mechanized Corps that were advancing west on both sides of Spassowo. The *Totenkopf* hit the right flank of the Soviet 5th Corps. Its armored group and the *III./"TE"* quickly reached Olympiadowka. On the other side of Ingulez the SS troops repelled the elements of three Soviet divisions that threatened its left flank at Tschetschelewika and Tscherwona Datscha. Fighting was bitter, but after noontime the bulk of the Soviet forces, trapped in the pincers south of Nowaja Praga, was finally cut to pieces west of Ingulez, leaving the hulks of more than seventy tanks littering the battlefield.

At 17:45 von Manstein ordered: *"Following the destruction of enemy forces in the Spassowo area, the next objective of 8.Armee is to attack as quickly as possible with three armored divisions of XL.Pz.Korps against the rear area of the 5th Guards Tank Army"*. Losing no time, the *Totenkopf* armored group left its positions on the night between 28 and 29 October, quickly clashing with a Soviet tank brigade. The T-34 tanks were engaged at short range, and within a few minutes at least fourteen Soviet tanks had been knocked out, while the SS troops incurred no losses. At dawn, the same SS troops attacked towards Malinowka.

A column of *PzKpfw.III* of the *Totenkopf* preparing to counterattack (*Charles Trang Collection*).

Soviet self-propelled guns attack.

The Soviets reacted by sending reinforcements in to the west of Ingulez. That morning the *Totenkopf* assault group continued its attack to the south, thus cutting off the escape route of the Soviet troops who were retreating. Completely disorganized, the enemy troops suffered heavy losses. The Soviets then made several attacks against the eastern flank of the *Totenkopf*, in the Federowka area. Soviet troops who were seeking to escape from the pocket also exerted strong pressure against the division's right flank.

All of their attacks were repulsed by the SS troops in violent fighting, which however kept a large part of the *XL.Pz.Korps* forces tied up in a secondary sector. At 13:15, General Wöhler telephoned General Heinrici: *"I am awaiting the conclusion of the battle of annihilation today, by 16:00 at the latest. After having regrouped, the bulk of the corps will attack towards the south"*. But, at 17:55, the vanguard of the *Totenkopf* found itself still stalled by strong enemy resistance in front of Tschetscheliwka. The Soviet bridgehead, which was stubbornly defended, could not be reduced. It was thus impossible for the *Totenkopf* troops to proceed onwards towards Petrowo. Nonetheless, further to the south, on 30 October the armored group of *14.Panzerdivision* succeeded in seizing Losowatka and establishing a bridgehead on the eastern bank of the Ingulez River.

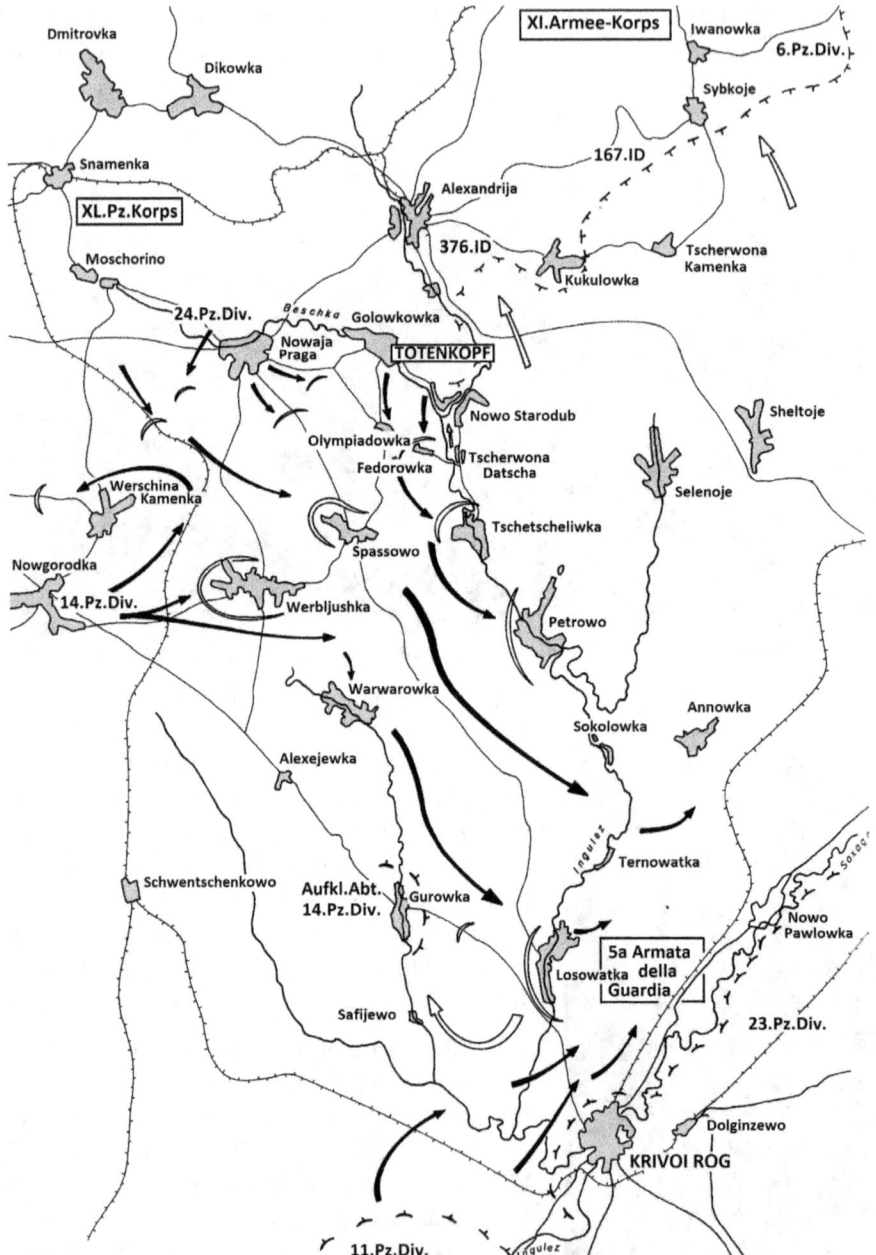

Fighting north of Krivoy Rog, Autumn 1943: the black arrows indicate German movements.

This same armored group was later joined by elements of 24.*Panzerdivision* at Ternowatka. It was a great success that closed the road to Krivoy-Rog to the Soviets. Once the gap was sealed, *XL.Pz.Korps* was expeditiously subordinated to *1.Panzer-Armee*.

A *Totenkopf* defensive position in the Fedorowka sector, Autumn 1943.

A *Totenkopf* officer in combat, 1943.

Meanwhile, *Totenkopf* troops completed a sweep of the western bank of the Ingulez, after which they finally reached the outskirts of Petrowo.

Fighting on the Dnieper

On 2 November, the *LVII.Pz.Korps* relieved the *XL.Pz.Korps*. At the same time, *Totenkopf* was ordered to prevent the Soviets from expanding their bridgehead at Petrowo. Its lines extended from Werschino to Petrowo. The next day, the SS troops were engaged in fending off numerous attacks by enemy forces. At 7:30, the destruction of at least fifty T-34 tanks was reported in the area east of Petropol. It was a success, but those early days of November were marked by departure of many of the division's officers. In fact, the *Totenkopf* division had to relinquish a part of its cadre to the *16.SS-*

Panzer-Grenadier-Division "Reichsführer-SS" that was then being constituted. The division had already suffered heavy losses during this period and this new bloodletting of personnel was a real disaster. In addition, those who left were among the best individuals with the most experience, such as Max Simon, Hellmuth Becker, Josef Maier, Max Dallinger, Fritz Knöchlein, Martin Stange and Walter Reder. In order to cope with this new situation, the division had to promote young officers to command positions.

SS grenadiers resting before resuming an attack, November 1943 (NARA).

A group of armored vehicles, *Marder II* and *SdKfz.250*.

In keeping with that, command of *SS-Pz.Gren.Rgt.6 "Theodor Eicke"* was assigned temporarily to *SS-Stubaf*. Kurt Launer and of *SS-Nachr.Abt.3* to *SS-Hstuf*. Wolfgang Borggrefe. On November 6, *LII.Armee-Korps* assumed control of the *LVII.Pz.Korps* sector, where fighting had decreased in intensity. The following day the *76.Inf.Div.*, coming from Italy, began to relieve the *Totenkopf* troops who had assembled in the area near Losowatka and Geikkowa. *SS-Pz.Art.-Rgt.3* and *3.Kp./SS-Pz.Jg.-Abt.3* remained in place and were attached to *76.Inf.Div.* to bolster its defensive capabilities. The *Totenkopf* profited from these days of relative calm to reorganize itself. Otto Baum, who had returned from convalescence, resumed command of the *"Totenkopf"* Regiment and Karl Ullrich was assigned to command the *"Eicke"* Regiment. On November 12, the German intelligence service announced a new Soviet offensive for the following day. However, weather conditions forced the Soviets to postpone their attack until the 14th: ten rifle divisions and four tank brigades overran the *76.Inf.Div.* positions and the right wing of *384.Infanterie-Division*.

SS engineers busy emplacing Tellerminen, November 1943 (NARA).

The army troops withdrew in great disorder. *I./SS-Pz.Art.-Rgt.3* and *3.Kp./SS-Pz.Jg.-Abt.3* managed to block the Soviet advance in front of Myschelowka. The *Totenkopf* was thrown into the breach. The panzers of *Gruppe "Biermeier"* intervened northeast of Myschelowka, where they surprised an entire Soviet tank brigade that was advancing single file: about thirty T-34 tanks were destroyed. Strong columns of Soviet infantry were similarly surprised southeast of Krassno-Konstantinowka. The panzers and *Flak* guns took a heavy toll. Around 14:00 the Soviets were forced to assume a defensive posture.

SS engineers busy emplacing Tellerminen, November 1943 (NARA).

SS-*Rottenführer* **Lothar Swierzinski.**

Between the *384.Inf.Div.* and the *76.Inf.Div.*, where the Soviets had opened a gap eight kilometers wide, the *"Eicke"* Regiment was engaged against two Soviet columns that were advancing parallel to each other. The strength of their attack pushed the SS grenadiers towards Bairak, where they dug in. All of the men were shifted to the front line, including the commander, Karl Ullrich. The SS troops succeeded in reestablishing the situation and retaking Hill 164.9, from which the entire sector could be monitored. A fresh Soviet attack overran the positions of the *III./"Totenkopf"*, opening a dangerous breach in the German defenses. In *10.Kompanie*, all of the officers and NCOs had been killed or badly wounded. It was a young twenty-one year old *Rottenführer*, Lothar Swierzinski, an former miner from the Ruhr, who assumed command in the field. This young SS corporal was able to scrape together the few survivors of his company, inciting them to counterattack. The grenadiers of *10./"Totenkopf"* fixed bayonets, yelled and charged the against the positions. Surprised by the unexpected attack, the Soviet soldiers fell back after furious hand-to-hand combat. Swierzinski himself was wounded in the encounter but refused to be evacuated, at least not until the captured position had been consolidated. A month later, having been wounded again in combat, *SS-Rottenführer* Lothar Swierzinski was recommended for the Knight's Cross, which he was awarded officially on December 16, 1943.

An *Sd.Kfz 250/1* armed with an MG-42 and an MG-34, November 1943 (NARA).

A *Totenkopf* grenadier (NARA).

Owing to this final defensive success, *LII.Armee-Korps* was able to announce that thanks to action by the *Totenkopf*, the breach opened by the enemy had been sealed. In reality, in the Bairak sector, where the Soviet advance had been stopped, the eight kilometer gap had not however been sealed. The *Totenkopf* was then given the mission to close it off by the following day. At dawn on November 15, Soviet artillery opened fire, following which fresh infantry and tank units were thrown into the battle. The lines of *Gren.Rgt.203* were penetrated northeast of Luganka. At 8:45 the *Totenkopf* sent an assault gun platoon to the area, which succeeded in destroying eight T-34 tanks and eight anti-tank guns, thus stabilizing the situation.

At Krassno-Konstantinowka, the *Totenkopf* faced off against the packed masses of Soviet infantry. Another assault gun platoon was called to the rescue and another eight enemy tanks were knocked out. Without tank support, the Soviet infantry suffered terrible losses and was stalled in front of the positions defended by the SS troops. The Soviets also attacked to the east of Bairak; the attacks multiplied throughout the morning and sixty Soviet tanks succeeded in penetrating the German lines. The SS soldiers let them pass so that they could deal with the enemy infantry. Losses were frightful on both sides: *8.Kp."TE"* had lost all of its officers and command of the company had to be assigned to an NCO.

SS grenadiers in an enemy position that has just been taken, November 1943 (NARA).

Meanwhile, a three kilometer gap had been opened in the "*Eicke*" Regiment's sector. The division then threw in all of its available reserves, in particular the assault guns of the

"*Köbel*" platoon and *Gruppe "Biermeier"*. Thanks to that support, the *III./"TE"*, led by *9.Kp./"Eicke"* under *SS-Hstuf.* Petersen, was able to counterattack and retake some of the lost ground. The Soviet penetration was thus eliminated and the front was temporarily stabilized. At 17:50, the *Totenkopf* was able to report to *LII.Armee-Korps* that it had destroyed more than seventy enemy tanks that day. This success, achieved while facing attacks by two armored brigades, a mechanized brigade, an assault gun regiment and seven rifle divisions, earned praise for the division by von Manstein, who at midnight sent the following telegram: "*Brave men of the Totenkopf, you are fantastic soldiers!*".

A *Totenkopf* armored group with half-tracks and a *StuG.III*, November 1943 (NARA).

An *Sd.Kfz.250* in an attack (NARA).

During the following days, the front line remained stable, despite the continuous Soviet attacks. It was not until November 21 that calm returned again. The *Totenkopf* had withstood all of the attacks and had destroyed a total of 241 tanks in the period between 14 and 21 November. However, its armored group was reduced to only three assault guns and a lone *Tiger* tank. By then, elements of the *8.SS-Kavallerie-Division*, commanded by *SS-Staf.* Streckenbach, were fighting on the right flank of the *Totenkopf*. On the right, the SS cavalrymen had to yield ground, losing contact with the *Totenkopf*. The fighting soon spread to the entire sector defended by the *Totenkopf*. At 19:50, the position at Krassno-Konstantinowka finally fell.

During the night between the 25th and the 26th, the *"Eicke"* Regiment organized a *Kampfgruppe* with all of the men who were available; twenty-five men from the headquarters and from the engineer company were scraped up. Their mission was to recapture Krassno-Konstantinowka, attacking against a force ratio of ten to one, but with the support of two assault guns and a *Tiger* tank. Incredibly, this handful of men was able to throw the Soviets out of Krassno-Konstantinowka.

A *Totenkopf* armored group preparing to attack, November 1943 (NARA).

The Knight's Cross for Felix Przedwojewski

During the defensive fighting in the Krivoy-Rog area, *SS-Uscha.* Felix Przedwojewski, born on 7 December 1920 in Meyenburg, an assault gun commander in *2./SS-Sturmgeschütz-Abteilung 3 "Totenkopf"*, distinguished himself in action. Przedwojewski had taken up a position along with two other vehicles of the *2.(StuG)Batterie* behind the grenadiers of *SS-Pz.Gren.Rgt.5 "Totenkopf"*. *SS-Uscha.* Przedwojewski was scanning the countryside when he suddenly spotted a formation of Soviet tanks, numbering about fifty, accompanied by many infantry about three kilometers from his position. The enemy force seemed to be headed towards the positions of the *"Theodor Eicke"* Regiment. *SS-Brigdf.* Priess had ordered Przedwojeski not to go into action before a formal order from him. The *SS-Uscha.*, aware that the spirit of initiative was fundamental in an elite formation, did not hesitate to shift his assault gun to a hill where he could better observe the enemy movement. The two other assault guns followed him. Przedwojewski was able, without being seen by the enemy, to close in on the

SS-Uscha. Felix Przedwojewski (BDC).

advancing Soviet columns. When the leading T-34 tanks got to within about two hundred meters, Przedwojewski gave the order to open fire. The first round was let loose; the leading Soviet tank took a direct hit and within seconds was a blazing torch. The other assault guns also opened fire, knocking out numerous enemy tanks.

Totenkopf grenadiers and half-tracks prior to an attack, November 1943 (NARA).

Totenkopf grenadiers around an *Sd.Kfz.250* (NARA).

With their ammunition exhausted, the three assault guns returned to the rear to reload and then quickly returned to their positions to continue the target shoot. In the end the Soviets lost thirty-four tanks to the guns of the three *StuG III* of the *Totenkopf*. A few days later, *SS-Uscha*. Przedwojewski succeded in destroying another ten T-34 tanks. *SS-Brigdf*. Priess cited him for the Knight's Cross, which he was awarded on December 16, 1943.

Clashes in the Bairak area

On November 27, the fighting shifted to the Bairak area. There the Soviets, following the heavy losses they had suffered during the preceding days, had adopted a new tactic, deciding to make heavy use of snipers to try to chip away at the German defenses.

An 81 mm mortar (*8 cm Granatwerfer 34*) of the *Totenkopf*.

Machine gun crews became their target of choice. The number of victims quickly mounted, after which the Soviets mounted a fresh attack that succeeded in penetrating the German positions on the boundary between *I.* and *III./"T"*. *SS-Ostubaf.* Otto Baum gathered all of the available men, including secretaries, radiomen and drivers, throwing them into the open breach: this new threat was eliminated in the early afternoon.

Totenkopf soldiers exchanching cigarettes, November 1943.

SS-Stubaf. Otto Baum.

A *Totenkopf Unterscharführer* (NARA).

At the end of the day, the division had the following operational vehicles: five *PzKpfw IV*, one *PzKpfw III*, one *PzKpfw VI Tiger* and two *StuG III*. The next day, the entire *LII.Armee-Korps* front was engaged in defensive combat. The corps headquarters ordered the withdrawal of the *I./"T"*, which was down to twenty-five *SPW* and about a hundred and fifty grenadiers, to constitute a mobile reserve. The bad weather and the deplorable state of the roads slowed all activity and offered the division a period of respite. Between June and November 1943 the division had lost 2,237 dead, 9,589 wounded and 409 missing, to which were added 2,408 sick who had been evacuated and 2,066 various other transfers. To offset that, it had received 5,197 men as reinforcements, to which were added 913 convalescents who had returned to their parent units.

In early December, eleven *Marder II* tank destroyers were assigned to the division, but only five were operational. There were twelve *PzKpfw III*, twenty-four *PzKpfw IV* and eleven *PzKpfw VI Tiger* tanks in the division's repair shops, but there were not enough spare parts to get them back in working order. On December 5, 1943, the Soviets resumed their offensive on the Ukrainian front, concentrating against the left wing of *1.Panzerarmeee*: Soviet armored forces overwhelmed the positions of the *384.Infanterie-Division*, whose mission was to defend the village of Federowka, northwest of Krivoy-Rog and then continued across open terrain seeking to cut the German lines of communications, beginning with that important supply center.

An *MG-34* on a *Totenkopf* half-track, November 1943 (NARA).

SS motorcyclists, 1943.

General Hube sent the *Totenkopf* division, which was dug in between the villages of Spasovo and Nova Praga, the following message: "...*Head to the south of Federowka and attack immediately*". Some *Totenkopf* elements were quickly dispatched to the front line. *SS-Kampfgruppe Masarie* was the first to be thrown into the gap that had been opened between *384.Inf.Div.* and the *376.Inf.Division*. On 7 December, all of the *Totenkopf* units that had joined action north of Dubowyj, *SS-Kampfgruppe Masarie*, *SS-Pz.Pi.-Btl.3* and *SS-StuG-Bttr.* "*Heinzmann*" were attached to the *384.Inf.Division* and placed under command of *SS-Stubaf.* Max Seela. Their counterattacks allowed the progress of the Soviet troops to be slowed down, but not to be stopped. Meanwhile, the bulk of the *Totenkopf* was engaged between Krassno-Konstantinowka and Rejewa Alexandrowka along a static front. On December 11, the division was attached to *LVII.Pz.Korps*. On December 13, several Soviet infantry units attacked the railway line west of Wassiljewska. The attack was stopped by the participation of four *Totenkopf* assault guns.

German grenadiers moving through a Ukrainian village, December 1943 (NARA).

A *Marder II* tank destroyer in combat, December 1943.

On December 19, *Totenkopf* troops were committed to a counterattack, along with *11.Pz.Div.* and *13.Pz.Div.*; the action was so swift that it caught the Soviets completely by surprise and stopped their advance cold. This allowed the Germans to reestablish a stable defensive front.

Fighting in the Kirovgrad area

The *Totenkopf* passed the end of the year in the area east of Gurowka. Although the sector was calm, its position on the front line did not allow the division to reorganize its forces or to improve its mobility. Only the assault gun group was able to be reorganized, and which once again numbered three batteries. On December 31, 1943, the division mustered 413 officers and 8,325 NCOs and

German grenadiers following a *StuG.III* during an attack.

other ranks. With respect to armored vehicles, there were five *PzKpfw III*, six *PzKpfw IV*, two *PzKpfw VI Tiger*, one *Bef.Pz.*, six *StuG III* and four *Marder II*. On January 5, 1944 the Soviets launched a new offensive further to the north, in the Kirovgrad sector. The *Stavka* plan was simple: surround and destroy *8.Armee* with the 1st Ukrainian Front, attacking from Chaschkow and with the 2nd Ukrainian front attacking in front of Kirovgrad.

A formation of *Pz.Kpfw.IV* tanks with infantry aboard, during an attack, December 1943.

SS-*Hstuf.* Anton Laackmann (BDC).

The Soviet forces were to link up on the River Bug, thus isolating *6.Armee*, whose destruction was to be the responsibility of the 3rd Ukrainian Front. In the face of this new imminent threat, von Manstein ordered the *Grossdeutschland* immediately to the Bobrinez sector, southwest of Kirovgrad, where it was to be subordinated to the *LIII.Armee-Korps* (*8.Armee*). It was to be preceded by a *Kampfgruppe* led by *SS-Stubaf.* Anton Laackmann, who had replaced Georg Bochmann as commander of *SS-Pz.Rgt.3*. This tactical group, consisting of *II./SS-Pz.Rgt.3* (with five *PzKpfw III*, ten *PzKpfw IV* and three *PzKpfw VI Tiger*) and *SS-Pz.Aufkl.-Abt.3*, was to counterattack towards Pokroskoje, through which the Soviet supply lines that threatened Kirovgrad passed. On January 7, *SS-Stubaf.* Laackmann's troops were subordinated to *Kampfgruppe von Gusovius* of *13.Pz.Div.*, commanded by *Hauptmann* Hans-Georg von Gusovius, former commander of *II.Pz.Rgt.4*. The attack kicked off at 6:00, under a thick mist, and with *5.Kp./SS-Pz.Rgt.3* in the lead. A Soviet column consisting of trucks and tanks was taken by surprise at the foot of a hill. However, many anti-tank guns came into action to slow down the advance of the panzers, inflicting heavy losses. At 11:35, *LII.Armee-Korps* ordered the attack to be suspended. The situation for the Germans was very critical: the Soviet 7th and 8th Mechanized Corps were on the verge of enveloping Kirovgrad and threatened to surround the *XLVII.Pz.Korps*. On January 8, the *Totenkopf* received orders to regroup its units in the Bobrinez sector. The relief operation began on January 10.

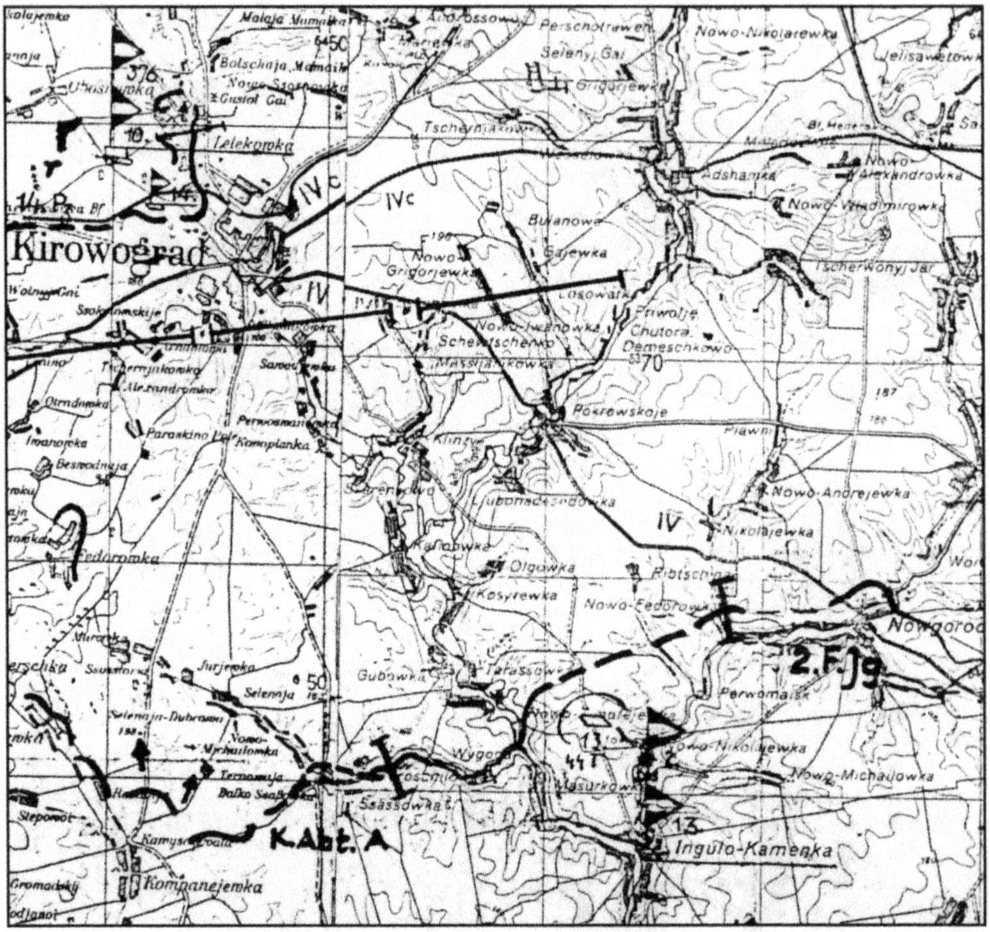

The area of fighting around Kirovgrad, January 1944.

A *StuG.III* ready to attack, January 1944.

On January 16, in freezing weather, the *Totenkopf* launched its counterattack north of Owsjanikowka, with the grenadiers on the right flank and the armored group on the left flank. Everything went according to plan until noontime. But around 13:00, Soviet artillery shelled the SS troops heavily while fresh troops were thrown into the battle, thus halting the German attack. In addition, the armored group was hit on its flank by a *Pakfront* and four *Tigers* were put out of combat. The SS troops were forced to dig in on the spot.

German tanks and grenadiers in a Ukrainian village, January 1944.

A *Totenkopf Tiger* Tank, January 1944.

Across the entire *XLVII.Pz.Korps* front, the Soviets lost 87 tanks and reported heavy losses, but nonetheless were able to penetrate the line of the *282.Inf.Div.* They had committed ten rifle divisions, an artillery division, two mechanized corps and elements of two tank corps. Under those conditions, it was imperative that the *Totenkopf* hold the positions it had just taken, pulling from the front a mobile unit consisting of *II./SS-Pz.Rgt.3, SS-StuG-Abt.3* and the *II./"TE"*, which was to be put at the disposal of the army corps. The next day the Soviets continued their offensive between Iwanowka and Alexandrowka. The *Totenkopf* was able to hold its positions during the course of bitter fighting. The *III./"TE"* and *StuG-Abt.3* had to hasten to the aid of the *10.Panzergrenadier-Division* at Andrejewka, where their counterattack threw the Soviet troops from the place.

The Axis Forces

A German armor formation during an attack.

A *StuG.III* of the *Totenkopf*, January 1944.

Discouraged by their losses and realizing that they would not be able to break through the German lines in that sector of the front, the Soviets called off their attacks at the end of the day. On January 18, defensive fighting continued in the area of Bogodarowka. On January 20 the *III./"T"*, led by *SS-Hstuf*. Zielke, arrived to relieve elements of the *10.Panzergrenadier-Division* at Andrejewka, while the *I./"T"* was busy fighting at Alexandrowka. The front was stabilized beginning on January 23. However, the Soviets were preparing to complete the encirclement *of XI.Armee-Korps* and *XXXXII.Armee-Korps* in the Korsun sector. All hell broke loose the following day in the area north of the front defended by *XLVII.Pz.Korps*. On January 25, the Soviets attacked the *Totenkopf* positions, taking advantage of a heavy mist. After having gotten close to the Germans, furious close-quarter fighting broke out. Losses for the attackers were high. The situation also became critical on the left flank of *XLVII.Pz.Korps*, where the 5th Guards Tank army had been able to open a wide gap. Between 26 and 27 January, this breach could not be sealed off, despite intervention by the *11.* and *14.Panzer-Division*. The Soviet 20th Tank Corps was now moving forward without meeting any resistance and the next day made contact with the forward elements of the 6th Tank Army at Swenigorodka, completing the encirclement of the bulk of *8.Armee*. On January 29, the Soviets shifted their efforts to the *XLVII.Pz.Korps* sector: the *282.Inf.Div.* was wiped out in a few hours and the loss of its positions opened a gap on the left flank of *Totenkopf*. The *III./"TE"*, supported by the division's armored group, left Petrowka around noon to counterattack. An anti-tank front was quickly destroyed. The tanks then made contact with the Soviet infantry, which began to flee in all directions. At 14:30, the division reported that the breach had been sealed. On January 30, the intensity of fighting in the *Totenkopf* sector decreased, as the Soviets shifted their efforts further to the north to strengthen their grip on Korsun. However, the division could not be relieved from its positions in order to be reorganized, because the *OKH* had no reserves to commit.

Bibliography
M. Afiero, "The 3rd Waffen-SS Pz.Div. Totenkopf 1939-1943: Vol.2", Schiffer Publishing

The Italian 8th Army in Russia
The First Defensive Battle of the Don
by Massimiliano Afiero and Ralph Riccio

Italian anti-tank position on the Don front, 1942.

In mid-August 1942, the Italian 8th Army, as part of Heeresgruppe B, was deployed along the Don, with the Hungarian 2nd Army on its left and the German 6.Armee on its right. Army headquarters had divided the defensive front into three sectors; from left to right were II Army Corps (294.Inf.Div., 'Cosseria', Ravenna), the XXIX.Armee-Korps ('Torino', 62.Inf.Div.) and XXXV Army Corps ('Pasubio', 'Sforzesca'). Beginning on 12 August, the Soviets began to make small-scale incursions against the Italian defensive line which cost a dozen or so killed and many wounded. The purpose of these actions was to find the weakest spots in the deployment and then to attempt to penetrate the line; one of these points was determined to be in the sector defended by the 54th Regiment 'Umbria' of the 'Sforzesca' Division.

Black Shirt troops on the march, August 1942. (USSME)

The Soviet attack

At 2:30 on 20 August, after brief preparatory fire by artillery and mortars, three regiments of the Soviet 197th Rifle Division crossed the Don on ferries and attacked the positions of the 54th Regiment of the 'Sforzesca', in particular, those of the II/54 on the heights south of Simovski and between Simovski and Krutovski and those of the III/54 between Satonski and Tyukovnoski. The Italians warded off the attacks twice. At 4:30, the Soviet attacks also hit the positions of the 53rd Regiment 'Umbria', at the boundary with the 'Pasubio' division near Pleshyakovski. At the same time the attacks intensified against the II/54 which was deployed on the right wing at Simovski, which soon found itself surrounded.

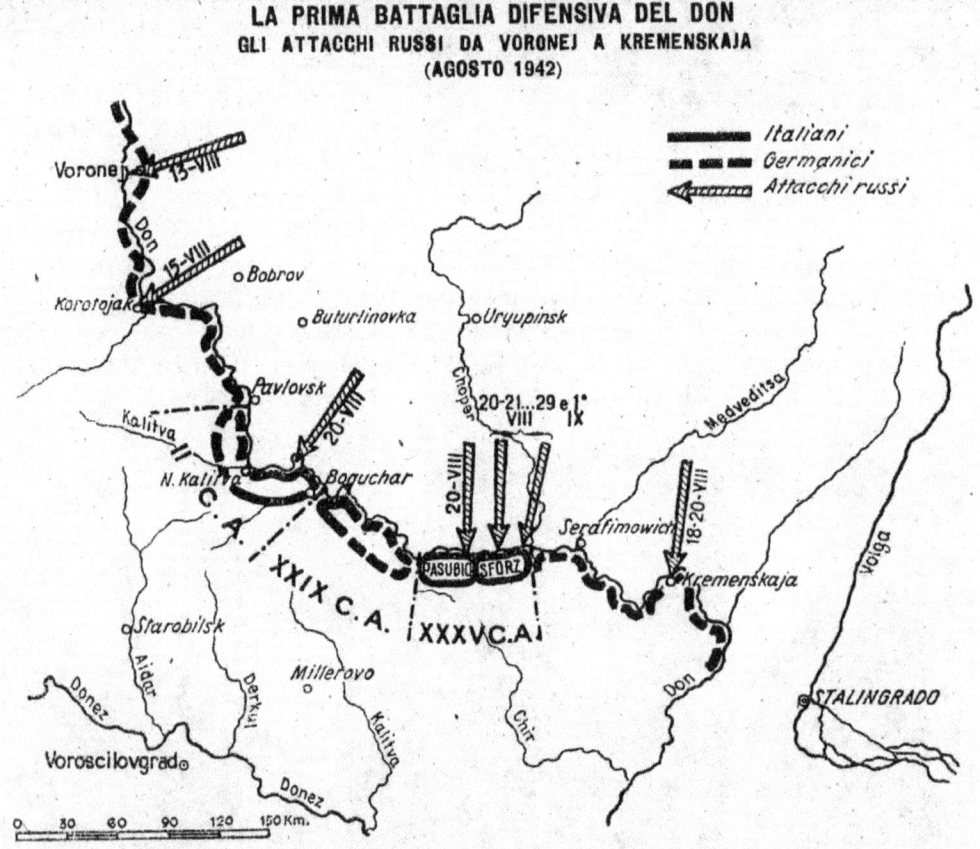

The First Defensive Battle of the Don: Russian attacks from Voronezh to Kremenskaya, 1942.

Division headquarters sent the battalion a company of the I/53 as reinforcement. At 7:30, XXXV Corps headquarters sent as reinforcements to the 53rd Infantry an antitank company and two flamethrower platoons, while to the II/54, which faced a greater threat, the LXII Battalion of the 'Tagliamento' Black Shirt group was sent as reinforcement; this battalion took up positions along the balka that from Krutovski ran from the Don to the southeast, managing to reestablish continuity of the defensive line and contact with the

III/54. At the same time, the I/54 was ordered to move to the north and to counterattack, aiming at Hill 163.1 and Simovski. Further to the right the Conforti column was engaged, which was to push to the north towards Bobrovski to protect the right flank that had been left exposed by German units. To add greater strength to the counterattack, General Messe also made available to the 'Sforzesca' the LXXIX Black shirt battalion, reinforced by the 3rd Battery of 75/32 guns. At 15:30, after desperate fighting that lasted at least twelve hours, the men of the II/54 were able to free themselves; of the 680 soldiers present at dawn, only 72 managed to cross back into friendly lines, moving to Hill 163.1 south of Bobrovski. The Soviet offensive thrust was temporarily kept in check.

A Breda 30 manned by Black Shirts, August 1942. (USSME)

Italian position on the Don front, 1942.

At 16:00, without the planned aerial bombardment against the opposite river bank, the I/54 mounted its counterattack, pushing Soviet forces back as far as Hill 142.4, while the 'Tagliamento' group and the 'Savoia Cavalleria' Regiment protected its flanks. A few hours later, fire from Soviet heavy weapons deployed on the right bank of the river stalled the counterattack about three kilometers south of Simovski. The Conforti column got as far as Bobrovski, but also was taken under enemy fire and was

Sergeant Major Eraldo Cabutto.

forced to withdraw. At the end of that first terrible day, Italian losses had been heavy, especially for the 54th Infantry. The continuity of the front line had, however, been maintained and a counterattack was planned for the following day to reestablish it completely. On the XXIX.Armee-Korps front, late in the evening, the 'Torino' threw back an enemy attack near Monastirshina. All of the attacks made against II Army Corps positions were also repulsed with minimum losses. Episodes of courage were not lacking, such as that of Sergeant Major Eraldo Cabutto of the 54th Infantry who, when he saw the Soviets break through the Italian defenses, gathered together a group of soldiers assigned to various service units, not from the front line, and leading them in a counterattack. Despite being badly wounded he refused to leave the front line, fighting to his death. He was awarded the Gold Medal for Military Valor posthumously.

Participation of the cavalry units

As previously mentioned, a counterattack on 21 August was planned by the 'Sforzesca' headquarters in order to stabilize the line of resistance along the Don; in particular, the I/54 was to attack on the right towards Simovski and in the center the III/53 and the XV Sapper Battalion were to move from Hill 190.1 and attack towards Nizne Matveyevski and Tyukovnovski while the I/53 was to attack towards Satonski and on the left, the II/53 reinforced by the 16th Chemical Company was to attack towards Pleshyakovski. But the

Italian cavalry units on the march, Summer 1942.

The Axis Forces

Soviets attacked first; after having had about a dozen infantry battalions cross the Don (elements of the 14th Guards Division and the 203rd Rifle Division), at dawn these forces moved to attack, preceded by preparatory artillery fire. The main Soviet effort focused mainly on the center of the 'Sforzesca' defensive front, against the III/53, which supported by two sapper companies, was able with great effort to hold its positions.

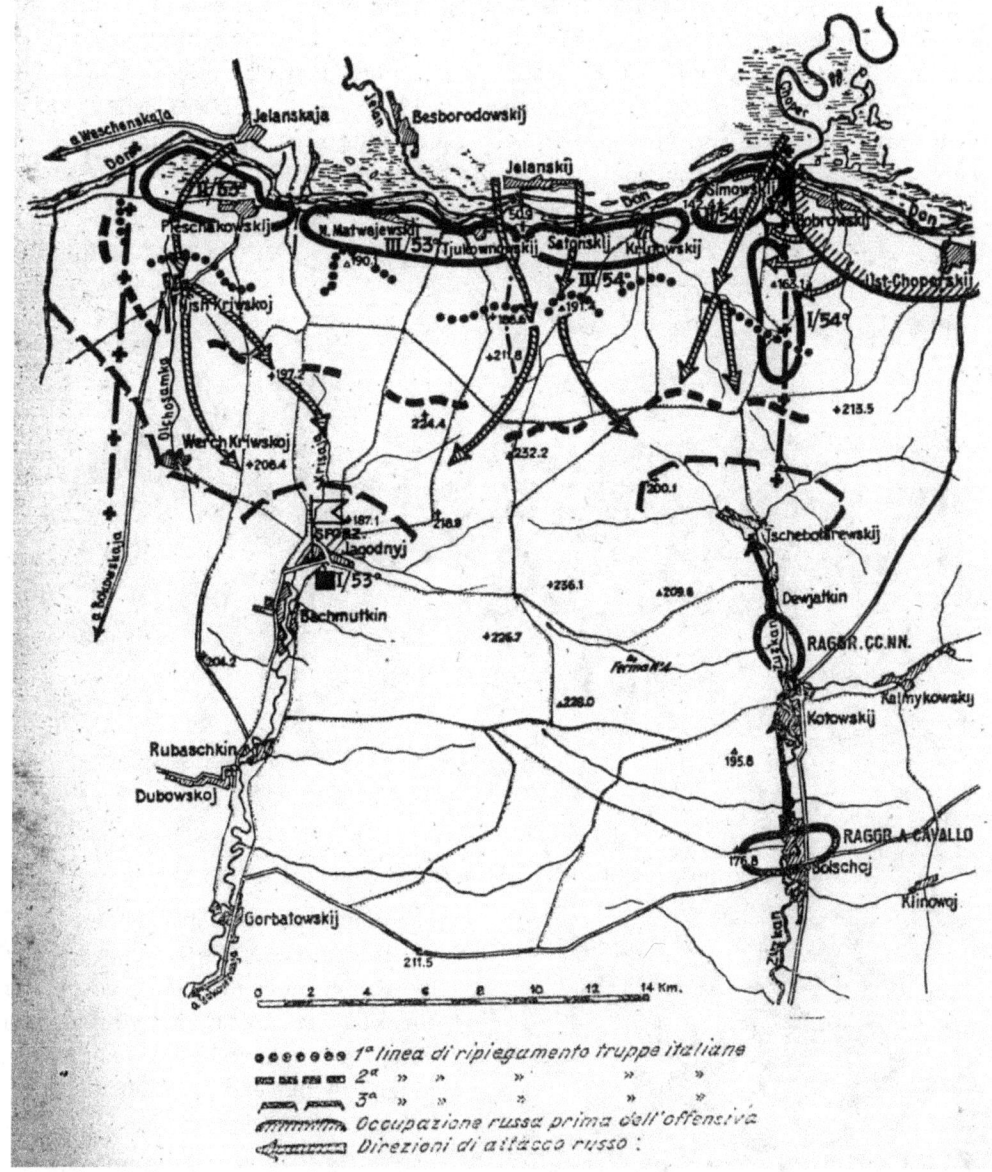

The First Defensive Battle of the Don: Initial attack in the Sforzesca sector (20-22 August 1942).

On the right, however, the planned counterattack was made around 7:00, even knowing that the action would not reach its objectives. At the same time, the counterattack against

Pleshyakovski was cancelled in order to defend the line of heights that dominated the Don. Around 10:00, the I Gruppo of 105/28 guns of the division's 17th Artillery, after having defended itself by firing point blank with its guns, was forced to withdraw, protected by the desperate resistance of the III/53. Shortly after, the infantry also pulled back, reestablishing some degree of continuity of the defensive line. In an attempt to close the gap that had been created between the two regiments of the 'Sforzesca', the Corps sent the LXXIX Black Shirt battalion of the 'Tagliamento', with orders to occupy positions between Hill 191.4 and Hill 188.6 to maintain contact between the 53rd and 54th regiments. However, during the advance, near Hill 193.7, the Black Shirts clashed with an enemy force and were surrounded. After managing with great tenacity to contain the attack, the Black Shirts fell back to the right-hand sector on Hill 193.7.

A Savoia Cavalleria patrol with Soviet prisoners, summer 1942. (USSME)

A mortar in action, August 1942 (USSME).

The ferocious resistance by the Black Shirts of the LXXXIX Battalion avoided the worst, preventing the Soviets from surrounding the right wing of the Italian deployment. The legionnaires fought to the end, as General Messe himself attested:

'Thus the LXXXIX Black Shirt battalion, which had been sent in the early hours of the afternoon from the extreme right towards the center of the divisional sector with the mission of establishing a new strongpoint, was attacked during its move by enemy forces dug in on the heights of Hill 232.2, a central point of the watershed between Kriutscha and Zuzkan. Heavily engaged from the front and at the time threatened on its right flank, the battalion heroically faced the critical situation: it is because of the knowing sacrifice of its soldiers that the enemy, due to having been stalled, was not able to overcome the right wing of the deployment until the late afternoon. The battalion, although with serious difficulty, was then able to withdraw.'

Cavalry troopers charging in an attack, summer 1942.

General Messe with italian soldiers, 1942 (USSME).

In order to stem the tide of the Soviet offensive against the center of the 'Sforzesca' positions, General Messe transferred and subordinated to 'Sforzesca' the horse-mounted units that were still available. Thus, at dawn the 'Lancieri di Novara' moved from Gorbatovo to Bakmutkin and to Yagodnyi, marching for 65 kilometers reinforced with mortars, antitank guns and a horse drawn battery group. The horse-mounted units, organized in two columns, with the Morcaldi column on the left and the Dal Re column (Major Dal Re) on the right, sent to support the 'Sforzesca' infantrymen, soon clashed with the advancing Soviet forces. The regimental commander ordered the recon detachment to take positions from the northern slopes of Hill 187.1, making contact on the left with the II/53, to the northern slopes of Hill 218.9, establishing contact on the right with the 'Savoia Cavalleria' Regiment. The horse artillery group displaced to southeast of Yagodnyi, while the regimental headquarters was in the same village with the rest of the available forces, grouped in the Pagliano column (led by Colonel Carlo Pagliano). The 'Savoia Cavalleria' Regiment was to be committed on the right of the 'Sforzesca', in the valley of the Zuzkan, where from the preceding day the Conforti column had already been in place and which at dawn on 21 August was engaged on Hill 163.1, along with the LXIII CC.NN. Battalion.

Cavalry troopers charging in an attack, summer 1942.

Colonel Alessandro Bettoni Cazzago, on the left, with the flag of the Savoia Cavalleria.

The rest of the regiment, grouped together in the Bettoni column, led by Colonel Alessandro Bettoni Cazzago and consisting of the regimental headquarters, II Squadron Group and half of the machine gun squadron, two antitank platoons and one horse battery, at 13:00 moved from Kotovski towards Ceboratevski. A patrol sent out on recon to Hill 232.2 found about a hundred infantrymen led by a captain, retreating in panic. General Barbò ordered them to deploy to new positions in the same area. Meanwhile the Bettoni column, on the march from Ceboratevski to the same Hill 232.2, clashed with Soviet troops and soon after assumed defensive positions along with an infantry unit that was deploying in defense of Ceboratevski. At 16:00, Messe officially attached the horse raggruppamento to the 'Sforzesca', which acting in concert with the LXXIX CC.NN. Battalion and two companies of the 53rd Infantry, was to reach the positions from the Hill 109.1 front to Hill 188.6. On the right the Conforti column was ordered to pull back, continuing to fight against the Soviets and at 19:00 set up along the new 'Sforzesca' defensive positions. During the night, the troops were consolidated on the two strongpoints at Yagodnyi and Ceboratevski. On the II Army Corps front, the troops of the 'Ravenna' division repulsed three enemy attacks, while the 'Cosseria' division was not attacked. At dawn on 22 August, deployed at the Yagodnyi strongpoint were the 53rd Infantry Regiment, part of the III/54, the remnants of the XV Sapper Battalion and the 3rd Flamethrower Company, for a total of about 3,500 men, with 71 light machine guns, 30 machine guns, 16 81mm mortars, 6 47/32 guns and 31 flamethrowers. The I/54 was gathering at the Ceboratevski strongpoint, while already present there were the II/54, part of the III/54 and the 'Tagliamento' CC.NN. Group, totaling about 1,000 men with 9 light machine guns, 21 machine guns, 27 81mm mortars and 2 47/32 guns. The 'Sforzesca' headquarters set itself up in Gorbatovo.

Poster from the first page of the period magazine *Cronache* Number 40 of 1943 which shows Lieutenant Mario Spotti leading his lancers in the "Charge at Jagodniy". (From a drawing by G. Bertoletti)

The charge of the 'Lancieri di Novara'

At 14:00, the Soviets attacked the Yagodnyi strongpoint, also attacking the positions of the 'Lancieri di Novara' between Hill 224.4 and Hill 218.9. Thanks to quick reaction by a squadron on foot (1st Squadron) which engaged the enemy frontally and by a charge on

Lieutenant Mario Spotti (www.movm.it).

horseback by another squadron, the Soviets were thrown back. The squadron on horseback was the 2nd squadron led by Lieutenant Mario Spotti who was ordered to charge against the enemy's flank. Shortly after 14:00, the 2nd Squadron advanced cautiously with its horses at a walk covered by a modest dip in the ground; as soon as they were out in the open, Lieutenant Spotti ordered the charge, shouting to his lancers: 'Boys! It's our day!. God and the standard are with us! Draw sabers…trot..gallop…charge!' The entire squadron of 100 men and 100 horses, as if on exercise with the points of their sabers at the oblique so as to hit from the top down, threw itself against the left flank of the enemy on Hill 224.4; it was unsheathed blades and horses charging against Soviet soldiers armed with automatic rifles, submachine guns and hand grenades. Lieutenant Spotti was among the first to be hit by enemy fire and although wounded, continued to charge while hanging on to his horse until, with his horse also hit, he fell in the midst of the Soviets who surrounded him and he continued to fight to the end with his pistol. The close-quarter fighting lasted only a few seconds. When his lancers, after a wild fight, managed to fell all of the enemy around him, they found him dead, his body and face marked by dozens of bullets and bayonet wounds.

With the lieutenant dead, command of the squadron was assumed by Second Lieutenant Mario Guerrieri, but the charge by the lancers, following the initial bold and overwhelming rush, had been transformed in the meantime into a series of ferocious close-quarter encounters. After having charged against the Soviet infantry with their sabers, the lancers were isolated amongst them in small groups. Most of them were surrounded little by little, with their horses knocked from under them by rifle fire or by bayonets. Many instances of bravery characterized this bitter struggle, which saw the Italian cavalrymen unhorsed and their mates rushing to their aid at the gallop, throwing back the enemy and helping them back into the saddle. In the end, Lieutenant Guerrieri and the 2nd Squadron got the better of it, putting the enemy battalion to flight. Losses for the 2nd Squadron were 1 officer, 1 NCO and 9 lancers killed, 24 wounded and 51 horses lost, of which 12 were killed. Lieutenant Mario Spotti was awarded the Gold Medal for

The Axis Forces

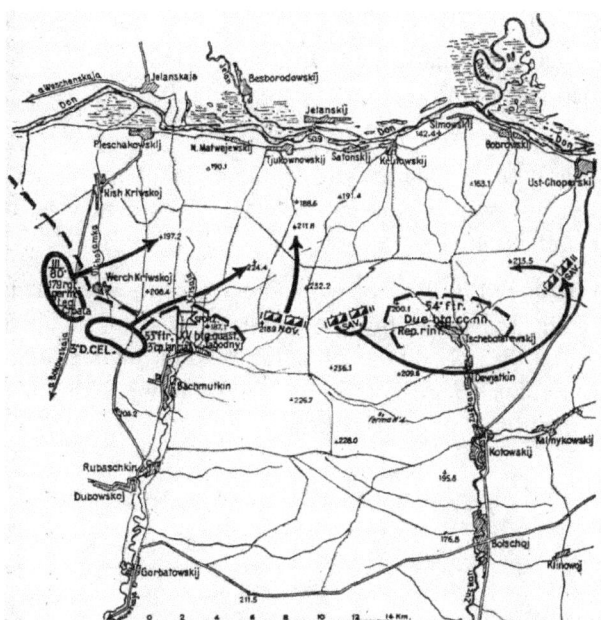

The First Defensive Battle of the Don: Italian counterattack (23 August 1942).

Italian bersaglieri during an attack, August 1942.

Military Valor. The truce lasted only a short while because the enemy returned shortly after, attacking with greater forces. Some Soviet units, after having managed to infiltrate in the balka of the Krisaya, were on the verge of taking Yagodnyi but were driven back thanks to personal action by Colonel Carlo Pagliano, who after having gathered all of the available men including horsemen, infantrymen, engineers and gunners, launched a counterattack. Around 18:00, the Soviets ceased their offensive action, leaving about a hundred prisoners and a large quantity of arms and equipment in Italian hands. The strongpoint at Ceboratevski was also attacked by the Soviets for about four hours, but without any success. More than 400 dead Soviets were counted in front of the Italian positions. In the afternoon, in addition to the 'Celere', the 'Monte Cervino' alpine ski battalion, the IX Engineer Bridge Battalion and the German Inf.Rgt. 179 were transferred to XXXV Army Corps.

The Italian counterattack

At dawn on 23 August, the Yagodnyi and Ceboratevski strongpoints were again attacked by Soviet forces but were again repulsed with heavy losses, thanks mainly to Italian artillery barrage fire. At the same time, to restabilize the situation on the right bank of the Don, a counterattack was planned, moving on the left of the 'Sforzesca' division's sector and that of the 'Pasubio' division. General Messe, who wanted to coordinate the action himself, had fixed the heights that dominated the River Don as the objective of the attack. Two columns were organized for the counterattack:

- a column on the left, under General Roberto Olmi, commander of the 'Pasubio' divisional infantry, consisting of the III/80, the Croat Legion, Inf.Rgt. 179 and two German artillery groups from 62.Inf.Div., which was to move from the area of Hill 219 to the west of Verhiniy Krivoskoy.

- a column on the right, led by General Mario Marazzani, commander of the 'Celere' Division, consisting of the entire division, which was to move from the area west of Bachmutkin towards hills208.4, 188.6 and 191.4.

The 'Monte Cervino' Batttalion, still deployed in the Gorbatovo area, was to take part in the counteroffensive on the right, while the horse raggruppamento was to join in to exploit the success. The attack began at 9:45: at 12:00 the left column, after having gotten past the balka at Olkovatka, occupied the village of Verhiniy Krivskoy and Hill 197.2, while the III/79 advanced on the ridge southeast of Rubeschinski.

Alpini of the Monte Cervino engaged in combat, August 1942 (USSME).

The right column attacked with the Felici column, led by colonel Ercole Felici, commander of the 3rd Bersaglieri, consisting of the 3rd Bersaglieri, with the XX/3 and XXV/3 in the lead, followed by two battalions of the 6th Bersaglieri and reinforcing elements. The Felici column advanced as far as Hill 208.4, where it was stalled by massive enemy barrage fire. In the early afternoon, the Italian troops skirted the hill from the east, reaching the area between hills 232.2 and 224.4, while the reserve units reached Hill 208.4 and the Otbelaize kolkhoz. At 16:00, XX and XXV/3 battalions attacked Hill 224.4, followed by the VI and XIII/6. The Soviets responded with massive barrage fire from artillery, mortars and machine guns. At 17:00, the summit of the hill was captured with bayonets and hand grenades. Meanwhile, the Salvatores column, which had just reached Hill 208.4, was attacked repeatedly and suffered heavy casualties. Further to the north, Inf.Rgt. 179 was also attacked on Hill 197.2; after having been pushed off the hill, the Germans counterattacked and retook the hill. In late evening, Colonel Felici had his troops withdraw further to the south, onto Hill 218.9. At the end of the day the losses were counted: the 3rd 'Celere' reported 28 killed (2 officers) and 263 wounded (17 officers), while the 'Pasubio' had 31 dead, 213 wounded and 65 missing.

Alpini of the Monte Cervino engaged in combat, August 1942 (USSME).

Bersaglieri engaged in combat, August 1942 (V. de Gaetano).

General Messe ordered the transfer of Inf.Rgt.179 to the 'Celere' and resumption of the attack against Hill 224.4, in three columns: Oberst Konrad von Alberti's Inf.Rgt.179 was to move from Hill 197.2, the Salvatores column (6th Bersaglieri) from Hill 208.4 and the Felici column (3rd Bersaglieri) from Hill 218.9.

Action by the cavalry units

Late in the morning of 23 August, General Messe had ordered the horse raggruppamento to focus on the enemy's left flank, moving to Hill 213.5, passing south and southwest of Tchebotarevski, in order to participate along with the 3rd 'Celere' in the capture of Hill 191.4 and then to proceed towards Krutovski. The 'Lancieri di Novara' were to reach Hill 191.4, passing Hill 232.2, but were only able to get as far as Hill 211.8. Threatened with being surrounded, during the night they pulled back to the area northwest of

Tchebotarevski. The 'Savoia Cavalleria' Regiment was to reach Hill 213.5 (situated about seven kilometers southwest of the village of Izbushensky) and the following dawn to move to Hill 193.7 so as to threaten the rear of the Soviet units that were pressing on Tchebotarevski and at the same time protect the right flank of the Italian deployment.

Italian cavalry deploying prior to an action, summer 1942. (Vincenzo de Gaetano collection)

Horse cavalry on the march, passing a horse artillery piece. (Vincenzo de Gaetano collection)

After having sent out reconnaissance patrols, it was found that the northwest slope of Hill 213.5 was occupied by strong enemy forces. With nightfall, the horse-mounted units made camp on the northern slope of the hill, bivouacking on the steppe and forming themselves into a square. The Bettoni column, led by colonel Bettoni Cazzago, consisting of the 'Savoia Cavalleria' reinforced with the II horse artillery group and by antitank guns (a total of about 700 men), while heading towards Hill 213.5, was spotted by the Soviets on the night of 23 August. Accordingly, to deal with the threat, during the night the Soviets shifted three battalions of the 812th Siberian infantry regiment of the 304th Infantry Division (about 2,500 men) to within about a kilometer of the Italian positions.

Italian cavalry deploying prior to an action, summer 1942. (Vincenzo de Gaetano collection)

Italian cavalry troopers on the move, August 1942.

The Soviets dug in between the sunflowers, forming a wide semicircle from northwest to northeast, waiting to attack the Italian troops.

The charge at Izbushensky

At first light, before moving to attack, a horse patrol was sent out, led by Sergeant Ernesto Comolli, to check out a 'suspicious' cart full of hay that had been noticed the prior evening in front of the Italian positions. A member of the patrol, Corporal Aristide Bottini, quickly spotted a soldier amongst the sunflowers. Initially, thinking of the presence of German soldiers, Bottini called out to him. But when the soldier turned towards them, they immediately spotted the Soviet red star on his helmet. Cavalryman Petroso immediately opened fire, hitting the enemy soldier in the head. The Soviets reacted promptly with massive mortar and machine gun fire which hit the Italian square and caused some losses; among these was Lieutenant Colonel Giuseppe

The Axis Forces

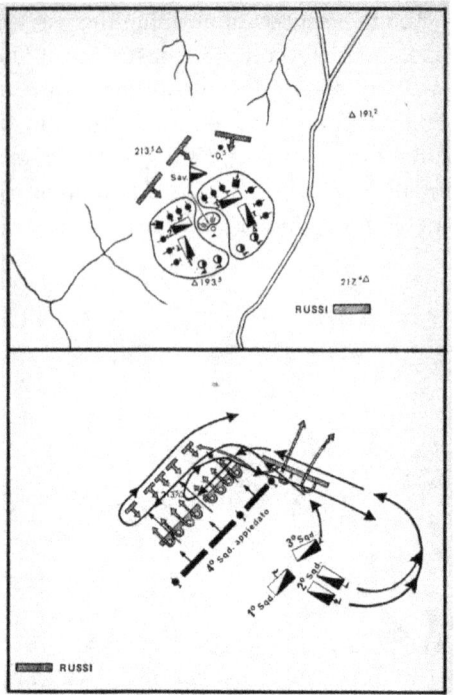

The battle of Izbushensky. At the top is the disposition of Russian and Italian forces during the night of 24 August 1942; below is a sketch of the movement of the opposing forces later that morning.

Captain Silvano Abba.

Cacciandra, the regimental deputy commander, wounded in the leg, and Captain Renzo Aragone, hit in the knee. The commander, Bettoni Cazzago, had a bullet go through his overcoat. Once having gotten past the surprise over the quick enemy reaction, while the squadrons were preparing to attack, the howitzers of the horse artillery battery, under Lieutenant Giubilaro, responded quickly to the fire, as did also the antitank guns and machineguns still in place from the night before. The prompt Italian fire forced the Soviets to lessen the intensity of their fire and to fall back on their own lines, which were too close to the Italian lines. Having noted the Soviet maneuver, the commander to the 'Savioa' decided to commit the 2nd Squadron on horseback into an attack, led by Captain Francesco Saverio De Leone, against the Soviet flank . After having made a wide detour, the 2nd Squadron fell upon the first Soviet battalion in close ranks and with sabers drawn, completely overrunning it and continuing the charge against the other two battalions. As the Italian horsemen passed them, many Soviet soldiers hid in their holes, then raising their heads and fire upon the cavalrymen from the rear. At that point, the 2nd Squadron doubled back, making a second charge, this time throwing hand grenades. The Soviet battalion on the left, before being overrun by the charge, was almost wiped out and its survivors, while withdrawing to the southeast, were captured by troops of the German 79.Infanterie-Division.

'The squadron came out of the slight depression in the ground unexpectedly, very close to the enemy's left flank; there was a moment of hesitation, followed by 'Galopoooo!' [Gallop], and right after that by 'Caricaat!'[Charge], a yell which was answered by a loud chorus of 'Savoia!'; the howl drowned out the din of the charge and was heard as far away as the regiment. The gallop then became an unleashed charge and the platoons erupted like a river overflowing its banks against the enemy lines, yelling, slashing with sabers, throwing hand grenades. The horses seemed to have overcome their tiredness and raged on in a froth, jumping over trenches and machine gun nests, heading in droves towards the objective indicated by the spurs and disappearing in enormous clouds of dust, followed by the noise of their hooves and by the furious chattering of weapons'.

Savoia cavalry troopers on the move, August 1942. (USSME)

First aid for those wounded at Izbushensky, prior to their transfer to a field hospital.

The other two Soviet infantry battalions, having suffered lighter losses, tried to react, at which point Colonel Bettoni had the 4th Squadron dismount, led by Captain Silvano Abba , and ordered it to engage the Soviet forces frontally in order to ease the pressure on the 2nd Squadron on horseback. The action was successful but Captain Abba was killed in the attack, hit by a burst of submachine gun fire while he was leading his men in the assault. Abba was later decorated with the Gold Medal for Military Valor posthumously.

Despite the two charges and the frontal attack by the 4th Squadron on foot, the other two Soviet battalions continued to fight back, inflicting notable casualties among the Italian troops. It was then that Major Dario Mansuardi, who had taken part in the 2nd Squadron's charge, went to Colonel Bettoni to ask for commitment of another horse squadron for a new charge. Accordingly, the 'Savoia' commander ordered the 3rd Squadron, under Captain Francesco Marchio, to attack. Joining the squadron in the attack were the commander of the II Squadron Group, Major Alberto Litta Modignani and his headquarters personnel.

Savoia cavalry troopers on the move, August 1942. (USSME)

Major Alberto Litta Modignani.

When, however, the 3rd Squadron went forward it reached a bottleneck between the folds in the ground and ended up coming under massive fire from Soviet machine guns and mortars well sited on the flanks. Following is testimony of Lieutenant Franco Toja: 'Seeing them arrive we stopped for an instant to watch that tremendous charge in awe, but soon fire fell upon them with incredible accuracy; I saw Ragazzi fall first, then Sergeant Mentasti, then Ardito, the major's orderly, then Sergeant Major Fantini who was riding Albino, then Sergeant Bonacina and Dossena and so many other troopers cut down like grain by the bursts. I saw Marchi who, bloody, cried in pain and in rage, and I picked up Bussolera who was wounded in the abdomen'.

Major Litta Modignani was wounded in the leg by a burst that had also killed his horse; the officer then tried to mount on his corporal's horse, but he was too weak. Dragging himself along the ground, he approached a machine gun position, pointing out to the machine gunner the targets to engage. He was soon hit mortally by another enemy bullet. Litta Modignani was killed in the charge, along with his aide, Second Lieutenant Emilio Ragazzi; both were later awarded the Gold Medal for Military Valor. Despite the heavy losses, in the end the charge by the 3rd Squadron put the last of the enemy to flight, pursued by saber blows and hand grenades; the two Soviet battalions were completely overrun and at 6:30 the battalion could be considered over. Captain Marchio was badly wounded in both arms

Second Lieutenant Emilio Ragazzi.

Colonel Ercole Felici.

and would later have his left arm amputated. The battle had cost the Soviets dearly, losing an entire battalion, with at least 250 killed and 300 prisoners in Italian hands as well as those captured by the nearby Germans. Many heavy weapons and machine guns were also captured. From the tactical point of view, the victory served to ease Soviet pressure on the Ceboratevski strongpoint and to free the position at Izbushensky, which was occupied by the Germans. It was only after the battle did it become known that the 650 'Savoia' cavalry troopers had clashed with 2,000 Siberian soldiers. Italian losses were 32 killed (3 officers), 52 wounded (5 officers) and about a hundred horses out of action. The 'Savoia Cavalleria' Regiment was awarded the Gold Medal for its banner, in addition to two posthumous Gold Medals, two Military Orders of Savoy, 54 Silver Medals, 50 Bronze Medals, 49 Military Crosses and several field promotions.

New defensive fighting

Thanks to the capture of Hill 213.5 by the 'Savoia Cavalleria', the posture of the XXXV Corps forces was improved considerably. However, Soviet attacks did not cease and at 13:00 three battalions of Soviet infantry attacked Hill 208.4, moving from the north and the east, supported by mortar and artillery fire. The men of the XVIII/3 and XIX/6 beat back the attack. However, the Soviets once again returned to attack the same positions for some hours, setting off attacks and counterattacks which cost the Soviets heavy losses: the 889th Rifle Regiment of the 197th Division came out of it almost completely destroyed. Around 21:00, the enemy attacks shifted to the 'Celere' sector, where another three Soviet battalions attacked Hill 219.9; with the cover or darkness, enemy troops broke into the positions defended by the XIII/6, taking the Italians from the rear. During the fighting, the commander of the 3rd Bersaglieri, Colonel Ercole Felici, was wounded, as well as two battalion commanders. Command of the 3rd Bersaglieri was temporarily assumed by Lieutenant Colonel Luigi Gianturco.

An antitank gun crew ready to open fire, August 1942. (USSME)

Alpini during an attack, summer 1942. (USSME)

At the same time, the Soviets attacked the positions held by the III/120 Artillery and the I/120 Antitank Artillery, whose crews defended their guns with hand grenades. The troops were ordered to withdraw to Hill 187.1. The bersaglieri of the 3rd Regiment defended this position to the last, all of the men dying with their weapons in their hands. The fighting also involved the II Corps sector; in particular, at 8:00 the Soviets attacked Krasno Orechevo, on the western side of the bend of the Verhniy Mamon, defended by troops of the 'Ravenna'. After two hours of fighting, the Soviets were able to reach the village; a counterattack by a battalion of the 'Cosseria' sent to reinforce the III/89 'Salerno' enabled Krasno Orechovo to be recaptured in the early afternoon. At dawn on 25 August the Soviets resumed their attacks against the sector that the 'Sforzesca' was sharing with the 'Celere', in particular against the strongpoint at

Tchebotarevski and Hill 209.6. The Tchebotarevski strongpoint was attacked from the north, east and west, clearly demonstrating the enemy's desire to isolate it completely. Its defenders, nevertheless, reacted well and were able to fend off the attack. The artillery gunners were however, forced to displace their guns to positions further to the rear.

Alpini during an attack with a Breda heavy machine gun, summer 1942. (USSME)

Bersaglieri inspecting a destroyed Russian T-34, August 1942.

Shortly after, the Soviets broke into Tchebotarevski, where house-to-house fighting broke out. The battle also spread further south to Kotovski, drawing anyone who could hold a weapon, including non-combat personnel, into the fight. The horse-mounted units were also caught up in the fighting in order to push back against the enemy attacks. General Messe requested assistance from XVII.Armee-Korps units, but no aid came from the Germans, despite the fact that a dangerous gap was opening between the Italian 8th Army and the German 6.Armee; if the Soviets had managed to capture Gorbatovo, they would have been able to envelop the strongpoint at Yagodnyi from the south and thus the left wing of 8th Army. Messe then decided to pull the defenses back to the western valley of the Kriuschya and to organize a new strongpoint at Gorbatovo, south of the Yagodnyi, to establish a defensive flank for all of the 8th Army and a base from which to mount a new counteroffensive across the Don.

Tanks of the LXVII Bersaglieri Armored Battalion on the move, August 1942.

A L6 tank of the LXVII Bersaglieri Armored Battalion.

During that same day, the forces of the 3rd 'Celere' were also attacked, beginning in the morning; initially the positions of the XXV/3 on hill 187.1 were attacked, north of Yagodnyi, but the Soviets were warded off. In the meantime, under protection of the alpini of the 'Monte Cervino' Battalion it was planned to withdraw Inf.Rgt.179 from Hill 109.2 to Verhniy Krivskoy. The alpini of the 'Monte Cervino' had also been engaged in the recapture of Hill 187.1 and when on 25 August they reached the positions which had been defended to the bitter end by the bersaglieri, they found themselves facing a scene that showed just how tenaciously the boys of the 3rd Regiment had fought: '...no one had evaded death, all of them had been massacred with bayonets, the machine gunners still had their fingers clutched to the triggers of their weapons that had run completely out of ammunition and in front of them were piled, one on top of another, the corpses of dead Russians...The alpini were joined by another small group of bersaglieri, and together they quickly moved up the hill, overcoming the resistance of the occupants using hand grenades'.

A 20mm Breda 35 antiaircraft gun position, August 1942. The 20mm Breda was an excellent weapon and was widely distributed to Italian forces. (Vincenzo de Gaetano collection)

General Gariboldi, second from the left.

Disagreements with the German headquarters

The withdrawals ordered by General Messe between 24 and 25 August, carried out to avoid destruction of the entire army corps, led to protests by Army Group B headquarters. To avoid any further withdrawal orders, the 'Sforzesca' division was subordinated to XVII.Armee-Korps. Messe protested this decision to General Gariboldi, which represented a clear lack of trust in the Italian commanders, but the 8th Army commander was able to do nothing. On the morning of 26 August, headquarters of XVII.Armee-Korps ordered the 'Sforzesca' to occupy a new stretch of the front line from Yagodnyi to Bolshoi. General Barbò, commander of the horse group, met with General Conradt, commander of XXXXIX.Gebirgs-Armeekorps to avoid shifting the Italian units, considering that enemy attacks were still in progress. At 8:30 on 26 August, numerous Soviet infantry attacked the positions of the 3rd 'Celere', first from the north and then from the east, but were driven back thanks to artillery support and action by Italian and German aircraft.

Bersaglieri motorcyclists engaged in tough fighting in a village, Summer 1942.

The Soviets resumed their attacks, attempting to circle around the Italian positions from the southeast; around 11:00, after having occupied the village of Bachmutkin, the Soviets continued to the southwest against Hill 204.2, threatening the artillery positions and the strongpoint at Yagodnyi. The XLVII Motorcycle Battalion was then thrown into a counterattack to retake Bachmutkin, moving from Hill 204.2, while the 'Savoia Cavalleria' group with the remnants of the II/54 and the 1st Motorcycle Company attacked from north to south. Caught between two fires, the Soviets withdrew from the hill and from the village of Bachmutkin, pursued by II Gruppo of 'Savoia Cavalleria'. In the afternoon, other enemy attacks developed against Hill 204.8 defended by the I/79 and against Ribni, defended by the III/79, all of which were repulsed. At the end of the day, 'Celere' losses amounted to 300 men killed and wounded. The Italians took 500 prisoners and a large quantity of heavy and light weapons. At dawn on 27 August, the eastern side of the Yagodnyi strongpoint was again attacked. After having been driven off, the Soviets attacked yet another time from the northeast, but were also repelled in front of the positions of the XXV/3 Bersaglieri. In the afternoon, the LXVII Bersaglieri Armored Battalion (consisting of two companies of L6/40 light tanks), recently arrived in Russia,

Alpini of the 'Monte Cervino' ski battalion in combat.

arrived to reinforce the 3rd 'Celere'. Towards evening, the Army Group B commander cancelled the order transferring the Italian units to XVII.Armee-Korps.

The Yagodnyi strongpoint

On 28 August, the Soviets attacked Yagodni from all sides with two rifle regiments, reinforced by a machine gun battalion and an NCO cadet battalion of the 213th Rifle Division. Also attacking from the north were elements of the 899th Rifle Division. The Italian positions were attacked from all sides, except from the south. After having managed to silence several Italian fire positions, thanks to artillery fire and a counterattack by the 3rd Bersaglieri, the Soviets were driven back after having lost hundreds of men, 400 prisoners and large quantities of equipment. Worn out by the fighting, the XXV Bersaglieri Battalion was replaced during the morning by the 'Monte Cervino' ski battalion. From the strongpoint at Gorbatovo, the remnants of the II/54 counterattacked against Hill 226.7, ejecting the Soviets. An attack by the II Gruppo of 'Savoia Cavalleria' followed against the left flank and rear of a Soviet column that was advancing on Bachmutkin, forcing the enemy to retire. In the afternoon, the remnants of the 'Tagliamento' group occupied Hill 288.0, taking the enemy by surprise and forcing them to withdraw. The I/54 was quickly sent to the hill to bolster its defenses.

The arrival of the alpini

The same day, 28 August, the Soviets also attacked in the 'Pasubio' sector against the positions of the II/79 in the area of Hill 188.8 and against Hill 204.8, defended by the Croat Legion. Both attacks were repulsed. Also arriving as reinforcements in the sector were the 'Vestone' alpine battalion, which joined alongside the 'Morbegno', both subordinate to XXXV Corps headquarters. Thanks to the arrival of these reinforcements a counteroffensive was planned which was to involve all of the alpine units of the 'Tridentina', the armored battalion and all other units present in the area. Participating in the action were also some forces from XVII.Armee-Korps. The attack was initially planned for 29 August, but on the evening of the 28th, the German headquarters reported that it would not be able to commit its own forces (22.Pz.Div. and elements of 79.Inf.Div.). The attack was then postponed to 1 September. Between 29 and 30 August, the Soviets continued to make attacks against the Italian positions, without committing large forces, and thus were all repulsed. In the evening of 30 August, the directives for the combined attack by Italian XXXV Corps and 79.Inf.Div. were established; the main objective of the German forces was the capture of hills 220 and 206.3, after which armored units were to continue on to Kotovski to make contact with the Italian units. XXXV Corps had as its objectives the ridge from Hill 236.7 to Hill 228.0, as far as the village of Kotovski, in order to make contact with the German armored units north of that village.

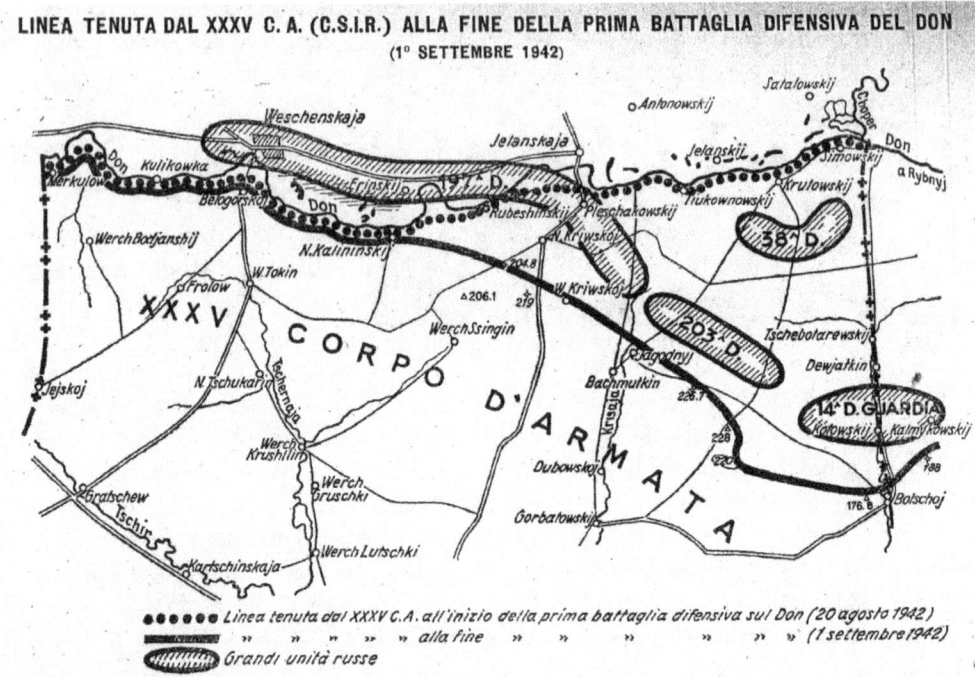

The line held by the XXXV Corps at the end of the First Defensive Battle of the Don (1 September 1942).

A defensive position of alpini on the Don Front.

The attack begins

At dawn on 1 September, after a brief bombardment by the Luftwaffe and by artillery, the Italian units moved to attack: the 'Vestone' alpine battalion advanced with its 54th Company against Hill 195.8, running into strong opposition. Its 55th Company, supported by the tank company, was able to capture the position of Ferma Number 4 at 8:00, making contact near Hill 195.8 with the 'Val Chiese' battalion which had come from Kotovski. With the Soviet troops in flight and having received the news that the Germans had occupied the village of Kalmikovski, the commander of the 6th Alpini Regiment, Colonel Paolo Signorini, ordered the 'Vestone' battalion to continue its attack towards hills 236.7 and 209.6. This latter hill was initially attacked by the L6/40 tanks, but strong Soviet fire caused them to withdraw. The assault by the alpini was more successful and at 10:30 the hill was captured. The Soviet attacks that followed were all defeated. At the same time, the 55th Company of the 'Vestone' surprised a Soviet battery on Hill 236.7; its crew were felled and four 76mm guns were captured. The attack against Kotovski by German armored units had not yet happened. Shortly afterwards, the news came that the German units, instead of occupying Kalmikovski, had halted at the edge of the village.

Alpine troops marching towards the Don, summer 1942. (USSME)

As a result, the company of the 'Val Chiese' battalion engaged at Kotovski was forced to withdraw and the other company of the same battalion that had already occupied Hill 178.1, after having suffered strong enemy counterattacks, was obliged to do the same. At the same time, the 'Vestone' company on Hill 236.7 was subjected to violent counterattack. To avoid having the bulk of the 'Vestone' surrounded, at 14:30 the 'Sforzesca' headquarters ordered the withdrawal of the units from hills 236.7 and 209.6. Particularly difficult was the situation of the L6/40 tank company of the LXVII Bersaglieri Armored Battalion: of the 14 tanks engaged along with the 'Vestone', six were damaged; of the seven tanks employed with the 'Val Chiese', two were damaged and five had jammed guns. Despite heavy enemy pressure, the withdrawal of the 'Vestone' was orderly, which allowed the alpini to bring the prisoners they had captured back to Italian lines. The battalion suffered the loss of 443 alpini (4 officers) dead and wounded. The 'Val Chiese' suffered 44 killed (4 officers) and 146 wounded (3 officers). The 54th Infantry of the 'Sforzesca' reported 21 wounded (1 officer). The action ordered by Army Group B to try to reinforce the linkage between the Italian 8th Army and 6.Armee was not successful, mainly because of the lack of help from the German armored units of XVII.Armee-Korps. With the 1 September action, the first defensive battle of the Don was concluded. For the Italians it was undoubtedly a tactical success, but losses were heavy. The battle also led to a profound crisis in relations between the Italian and German headquarters, mainly because of the initial dissolution of some of the 'Sforzesca' troops, accused of having abandoned their positions without fighting.

Bibliography
Massimilano Afiero & Ralph Riccio, "*Snow, Ice and Sacrifice. The Italian Army in Russia 1941-1943*", Helion & Company Limited

Sprungeinsatz Monterotondo 9-10 of September, 1943
by Guido Ronconi

After the declaration of "war state" of the siege of the military high commands in January 1943, in May-June 1943 the General Staff of the Royal Army (SMRE) was transferred to the country headquarters in locations around Rome, in particular the offices of the Chief of Staff of the Army and of the Sub-Chiefs for Operations and Intendant were headquartered in Monterotondo (code Centro Marte). Monterotondo, a town located about 20 kilometers north of Rome, therefore found itself hosting the most important offices of the SMRE in the Orsini castle, located in the center of the town, and therefore became a Military Place under the command of Col. Giuseppe Angelini, becoming the object of notable fortification works. The area was in fact suitable for a paratroop drop, however the defensive works and the organization of the garrison were structured to cope with attacks conducted by land and not from the air, and this in line with the increasingly probable eventuality of a change of alliances by Italy, which would have meant that the danger would have come from the German ground forces and no longer from Allied airborne landings. Angelini organized the defenses of Monterotondo on three lines: an external defense centered on 5 strongholds to control the access roads to the town, each consisting of a bunker with a 75/27 piece in anti-tank function and several machine gun positions in barbette, a internal defensive wall based on anti-tank walls protected by machine guns blocking the accesses to the city center and various machine gun positions and finally a central redoubt, namely the Orsini castle, which dominated the city center.

The Orsini castle seen from the Cappuccini convent as it appeared in September 1943 (Wolfgang Stocker/ECPAD).

Furthermore, the strongholds on the Via Nomentana, north and south of Monterotondo, were protected by minefields and also had 2 90/53 autocannons with anti-tank purposes.

The 75/27 pieces arranged in the 5 bunkers belonged to the 481st Battery with 2 officers, 6 NCO and 41 artillerymen. Among the particularly important defensive preparations were the emplacements for the pieces of the DIII AA Mixed Group, with a total of 30 officers and 700 artillerymen whose 90/53 truck-mounted guns had a dual anti-tank and anti-aircraft function. The 1st Battery was deployed with three pieces in anti-aircraft purposes to the west of the San Luigi area, with a fourth piece detached on the Via Nomentana north of Monterotondo, while the 2nd Battery, with three pieces, was located on Monte Oliveto, a hill east of the town, in anti-aircraft function, its fourth piece was integrated into the Nomentano stronghold with anti-tank function.

Men of the Motorized Assault battalion during an exercise near Monterotondo: second lieutenant Mario Fichelett standing in the centre. (Arch. R. Gavirati)

The distance between the two batteries allowed them to cover each other in case of air attacks. In addition to the XXXI Sappers Battalion, made up of around 600 men, there was a Company from the HQ. of the SMRE with about a hundred men, the 9th Mixed Grenadier Company, a hundred men with an exceptionally heavy armament of 20 Breda heavy machine guns assigned to occupy the numerous barbette machine gun positions, and the 2nd Company of the Autonomous Group of the Carabinieri by the SMRE, strong of around 180 men of which a section of 32 carabinieri with 3 heavy machine guns and 8 light machine guns under the command of Lieutenant Vessichelli had been assigned to the defense of the Orsini castle. For maneuver defense the Motorized Assault Battalion of 3 companies was available. On the evening of 8 September, two companies left Monterotondo to escort the SMRE column moving to Rome. Only the 2nd Cp. remained in Monterotondo, with around 100 men under the command of Capt. Michele Cassano. The forces available to Angelini, at the time of the German attack amounting to approximately 1750-1800 men, were therefore considerable and, despite without armored vehicles, adequate for the task of defending the SMRE for a few hours while waiting for reinforcements coming from the units stationed at Rome. In Monterotondo there were many other hundreds of soldiers, both in service at the SMRE and assigned to other bodies and tasks, with limited combat value.

The German plans

On the evening of 25 July 1943, shortly after the news arrived that the session of the Grand Council had led to the fall of fascism and the arrest of Mussolini, a meeting was held at Hitler's headquarters, attended by the major German military leaders, in which the Führer decided to immediately occupy Rome and arrest the members of the government, the highest military leaders and the entire royal family. Hitler commissioned the General Student, commander of the XI. Fliegerkorps, to immediately transfer all the available parachute troops near Rome in order to maintain control of the city at all costs and prevent the German units engaged in the South from remaining isolated, he also ordered him to free Mussolini and capture the major political and military leaders Italians as well as the royal family, with the aim of re-establishing a fascist government (*Unternehmen "Schwarz"*) . However, on the following 31 July Student clashed with the contrary opinion of OB Süd Feldmarschall Kesselring, convinced of the illegality of the "*Schwarz*" operation, which was cancelled. However, the immediate transfer of the 2nd Fallschirmjäger-Division from southern France to Italy had already been ordered and on 26 July the parachute division suddenly arrived by air, without prior authorization from the Italian side, at Pratica di Mare airport and took up quarters in Castelfusano, near Rome.

The anti-tank wall located at the entrance to Monterotondo near today's via Federici (Wolfgang Stocker/ECPAD).

The II. Bataillon/Fallschirmjäger-Regiment 6, under the command of Major Walter Gericke, did not follow the rest of the division: the battalion on board 52 Junkers 52 transport planes continued to Manfredonia, where they waited among the olive trees. The transport planes remained with the battalion, thinned out and camouflaged among the trees, ready to go into action immediately. Gericke was then summoned by Student to his HQ. of Frascati; Student immediately got to the point and explained the reason for the summons, namely "to capture the Italian Headquarters with an airborne action and thus paralyze the entire command system of the Italian army. For this task he must rely only on himself. For reasons of secrecy, no help can be given to her either before the launch or during the fight". Gericke then returned to Puglia, with the onerous task of planning an airborne operation on a target whose characteristics were practically unknown. While his men trained hard for the imminent action, Gericke took care to acquire sufficient information on the objective to effectively plan the launch of his battalion, while maintaining absolute secrecy. After a failed attempt to fly over Monterotondo aboard a Fieseler Storch, Gericke pretended to have to cross the town to meet a phantom regiment coming along the Via Salaria. On the return journey, left free to cross Monterotondo without surveillance by the Italians, Gericke had the opportunity to observe and imprint in his mind the details and particularities of the places and the defensive preparations. Furthermore, a few days later he received from Student headquarters the aerial photos that had been promised to him and which allowed him to develop the attack plan. The launch should have taken place in such a way as to immediately isolate the castle and prevent the occupants from escaping, so as to be able to trap and capture Gen. Roatta and, as some paratroopers thought, Badoglio too! Therefore the launch of the four companies would have been as close as possible to the Orsini castle, so as to land behind the Italian defensive works, arranged in such a way as to defend Monterotondo from an attack coming from the outside. The launch zone planned for the 5. Kompanie was located north-east of Monterotondo, near the stadium, the 6. Kompanie was supposed to land on the northern edge of the town, the launch zone for the 7. Kompanie and the Stabskompanie was instead planned to the south of the town near the Capuchin convent while the 8th. Kompanie should have landed on the road to Mentana.

September 8

On the afternoon of September 8, a few hours before the announcement of the armistice on the radio, Roatta issued the order to transfer the SMRE to Rome, therefore on the night between 8 and 9 September the columns of vehicles loaded with material they set off towards Rome, escorted by two out of the three companies of the Motorized Assault Battalion and by the 2nd Cp. CC.RR., who left in Monterotondo only a nucleus of around seventy carabinieri including the 32 men assigned to the defense of the Orsini castle. Part of the vehicles used for transport should have returned to Monterotondo to complete the transfer of personnel, but once in Rome they were partly sent to other destinations. This meant that in Monterotondo on the morning of the 9th there were still many officers and soldiers of the SMRE, mostly of little combat effectiveness, waiting in vain for the trucks. Upon hearing the news of the armistice, Gericke summoned the company commanders and in their presence, having finally managed to get in touch with Student, he repeated the general's words aloud: "The betrayal of Badoglio and the royal house has manifested itself! Act on your own initiative!", therefore Gericke addressed his company commanders with these words: "Departure tomorrow morning at 6.00! Drop on Monterotondo, Italian headquarters! You already have the aerial photos!".

Dawn of 9 September 1943: the ground personnel of the Transportgeschwader 4 observe the taxiing and take-off of the Ju.52 with the paratroopers of II./FJR 6 on board heading to Monterotondo (Author's collection).

Dawn of 9 September 1943: Oberleutnant Thomsen, commander of the 7.Kompanie, will prepare for take-off (Author's collection).

The takeoff of the 50 Ju. 52 began at 6.30. One plane had to land in emergency and did not reach the objective, the other 49 with 650 paratroopers on board arrived on the Monterotondo vertical at 8.20.

September 9

The Italian anti-aircraft units initially identified the Ju. 52 as American planes as they were coming fron South, but as soon as the misunderstanding was clarified they opened fire which immediately proved effective and led to the shooting down of a Ju. 52 and the damage to at least two others. Despite careful planning, errors occurred in the launch: the 6th and 7th Kp. they touched land about 2.5 km north of the planned area, between the bend of the Tiber and Monterotondo Scalo. Some elements even landed north of the Tiber, but the Ju. 52 returned to fly over them and launched them with the life boats supplied which allowed some of the paratroopers to immediately cross the river and rejoin their units, while those who landed further away went north to cross the Tiber at the Grillo bridge. At 5.00 on 9 September a convoy arrived in Monterotondo Scalo with the commander of the 2nd Rgt. Ftr. of the "Re" division, Col. Edmondo De Renzi, the HQ Company, made up of 15 officers and 243 NCOs and troops, and the Regimental Infantry Guns Battery with 4 65/17 pieces, the vanguard of the division transferring from Croatia. From a brick factory, approximately 150/200 sappers belonging to the 638th and 639th Workers Companies, engaged in works on the railway line, opened fire on the paratroopers.

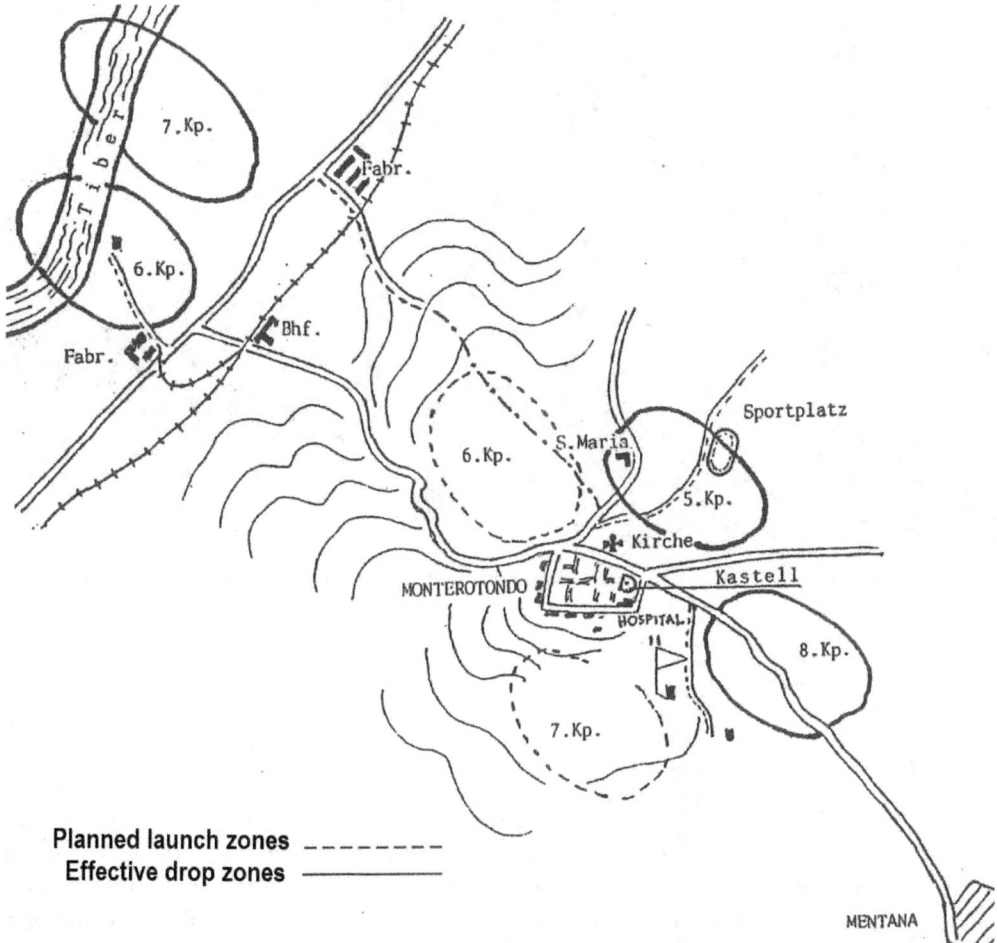

Map of the Monterotondo area with the indication of the drop zones of the German paratroopers (from D. Brehde, *Der Blaue Komet*).

As soon as they gathered and realized the new, unexpected tactical situation, the paratroopers immediately attacked the railway station and the brick factory. The sappers barricaded in the factory soon gave up and were captured, allowing the paratroopers to attack the station and begin to infiltrate the sides of Via Nomentana in the direction of Monterotondo. The launch of the paratroopers had taken the men of the "Re" by surprise, but De Renzi and his officers took the situation into their own hands and gathered around 250 "red ties" who, stationed behind the railway embankment, began to target the Germans with individual weapons. De Renzi, realizing that the Germans' objective was the SMRE's HQ, deemed it appropriate to retreat with around 200 men to the hills southeast of the station and try to join the Monterotondo garrison, while a contingent of around 50 men had the task of containing the German attack on the station, a task only partially carried out due to the sudden wounding of the commanding officer.

The main entrance of the Orsini castle photographed a few days after the fighting (Wolfgang Stocker/ECPAD).

The 90/53 autocannon on Breda 51/52 chassis of the 2nd battery of the DIII Gruppo Misto C.A. placed in an anti-tank position near the bunker on Via Nomentana (Eugen Gremelsbacher/ECPAD).

Having occupied the station and disarmed the prisoners, the Germans began to advance towards Monterotondo, with the 7th Kompanie to the north and the 6th Kompanie to the south of the Via Nomentana, hindered by the fire of the 1st Btr. from 90/53 guns belonging to the DIII A.A.Mixed Group. Going up the tortuous route of the Via Nomentana towards Monterotondo, the paratroopers bypassed and left the battery positions behind and continued towards the town. Having overcome the last obstacles, namely the checkpoint at Villa Frontoni and finally the anti-tank wall and the bunker at the entrance to the town, at 1.00 pm, with approximately 4 hours' delay, the two companies finally reached Monterotondo and made contact with the 5 Kp. which had meanwhile reached the Porta Garibaldi area. The paratroopers landed on the right bank of the Tiber came into contact with Stronghold H, located in Osteria del Grillo with the task of controlling the Grillo bridge on the Tiber, made up of units of the "Piave" division: the 2nd Cp./I Battalion. /57th Ftr. Regiment under the command of Capt. Radin and strong of about 110 men, and the 7th Btr./III Gr./20th Rgt.Art. with 4 pieces of 75/27.

Some paratroopers meet the Italian prisoners coming from Porta Garibaldi (Bundesarchiv).

An Italian 20 mm machine gun in action in Monterotondo (from *Roma in Guerra*).

Following the order from the Motorized Armored Army Corps (Corpo d'Armata Motocorazzato, CAM) that same morning to the "Piave" division to abandon all strongholds and move to the Tivoli area, Radin's men had left their positions and, mounted on trucks, were waiting the moving order when the paratroops' drop prompted Radin to order his men to reoccupy their positions. Attacked shortly afterwards by the Germans, the infantrymen of the "Piave" prevented them from crossing the Tiber while maintaining control of the Grillo bridge, an element that would prove to be of fundamental importance the following afternoon. The 5.Kompanie landed near the stadium, where there were

The Axis Forces

10 September: during the truce of arms in the courtyard of the Orsini castle, Major Gericke, in the centre, and his orderly officer, Second Lieutenant Christiansen, on the right, meet Major Trombetta, commander of the I/57th (BA).

barracks housing the soldiers of the Garrison and on duty at the SMRE. After a brief firefight the paratroopers captured the Italian soldiers and, locking them up in the barracks and leaving a few men to guard them, continued in the direction of Monterotondo. A group of 8 paratroopers under the command of Ltn. Brehde, having landed near the town, moved quickly towards the castle and, taking the captured First Lieutenant Vessichelli with him as a guide, reached the Orsini castle at 9.00, not even half an hour after the launch, but was nailed down in the overlooking gardens by machine gun fire coming from the castle: the surprise had failed! The bulk of the 5. Kompanie moved from the stadium in the direction of the town: although hindered by the fire coming from the HQ of the DIII A.A. Mixed Group, stationed at Villa Federici, the paratroopers did not attack it, concentrating instead on eliminating the two bunkers placed on their itinerary. Having taken possession of a 75/27 gun, they pushed it by hand towards Porta Garibaldi and used it to target the slits of the anti-tank wall, thus allowing two paratroopers to place explosive charges at the foot of the wall, thus creating a breach through which they could pass and stop in front of Porta Garibaldi: it was around 11.00, the 5. Kp. stopped and continued to exchange gunfire with the Italian troops barricaded in the historic center, but did not attack while waiting to establish contact with the other Kompanien. The 8. Kompanie landed in the expected area, near the Capuchin convent. The paratroopers immediately occupied the Navy radio station, but the platoons that descended close to the wall that bordered the Capuchin garden immediately found themselves in a bad situation. Here was in fact the 2nd Cp. of the Assault Battalion which, under the command of Capt. Cassano and with weapons at the ready, awaited the arrival of the vehicles that were to take it to Rome. After an initial moment of disorientation, the Italians set out to defend themselves and, protected by the surrounding wall, began to target the Germans who, stuck in the open, found themselves in difficulty. Cassano, however, in a moral crisis due to the sudden change of alliances, opted to make contact with the German commander through a captured paratrooper and after a brief discussion decided to cease hostilities. The Germans obviously didn't loose any time, they took everyone prisoner and after locking them up in an adjacent building they began to advance quickly in the direction of the hospital and the bunker guarding the street coming from Mentana.

10 September: in the square in front of Porta Garibaldi some paratroopers of the 5.Kompanie listen to their commander, Oberleutnant Siegfried Nitzschke, flanked by Leutnant Schiedewitz, on his left (Bundesarchiv).

September 10: the truce of arms is underway and Italians and Germans are fraternizing.

Having neutralized the bunker and taken possession of the 90/53 autocannon, which was immediately used against Villa Federici, the paratroopers partly prepared to defend themselves in the direction of Mentana, to block any Italian attempt to bring aid to the troops located in Monterotondo, and partly moved towards the Orsini castle: attacking with the usual decision they overwhelmed the Italian defenses and arrived at the castle gardens, where they were blocked by fire coming from the building, and near Porta Garibaldi, where shortly afterwards they joined up with the 5th Kp. coming from the stadium. Col. De Renzi, having left a covering force at the Monterotondo station, took himself with around 200 men and six officers to the hills east of the station, in the Vallagati area. Taking advantage of the guidance of a local boy,

Dario Ortenzi, the units of the 2nd Rgt. Ftr. he arrived around 10.00 at the stadium where the Italian soldiers captured by the paratroopers were locked up. De Renzi decided to attack the Germans on guard: De Renzi himself and three of his officers, leading a handful of men, penetrated the fence surrounding the stadium and after a brief fight put the paratroopers to flight, thus freeing the prisoners.

German paratroopers control a group of civilians among whom soldiers from the Royal Army could be hiding (Bundesarchiv).

10 September: paratroopers of the 5.Kompanie in the square in front of Porta Garibaldi (Bundesarchiv).

Then De Renzi with his men and a part of the freed prisoners joined the command of the DIII A.A. mixed group at Villa Federici. Here he learned that the SMRE was no longer present at the Orsini castle, therefore he considered it useless to attack the Germans in Monterotondo and preferred to establish himself as a stronghold in the villa, sustaining firefights with the paratroopers for the rest of the day.

The Orsini castle is taken

As soon as they noticed the launch, the carabinieri rushed to the castle, so that when the paratroopers arrived in the city center the defense was already organised, reinforced by other soldiers serving at the SMRE and remaining for various needs in Monterotondo. After several unsuccessful attempts to communicate the German attack to the commands in Rome, the garrison finally managed to contact the SMRE offices in Tivoli: Col. Montezemolo, coincidentally present there, promised to send reinforcements as soon as possible. During the morning at least two parliamentarians were sent by the paratroopers to demand the surrender of the garrison, but the requests remained unanswered. It was therefore clear to the Germans that the castle could only be conquered with a concentric attack from all sides, possible only after the reunification of the four Kompanien in the city center, which occurred at 1.00 pm on the edge of the town.

On the square in front of Porta Garibaldi, in front of the church of San Rocco, Oberleutnant Ernst Knuss, commander of the 6.Kompanie, talks to his men (Bundesarchiv).

Accustomed to acting autonomously and with the objective of occupying the Orsini castle always in mind, the commanders of the Kompanien, unable to make contact with Gericke, decided to attack and occupy the historic center of Monterotondo in order to reach the castle also from the sides west and south, and then carry out a concentric attack. The 7. Kompanie, with contained losses despite the initial, strong Italian reaction, reached the positions envisaged by the original plan, i.e. to the south and south-east of the castle. The 6. Kompanie moved from the positions near the current Federici street: the platoons headed directly towards the west side of the castle through the city center, where they had to fight their way through. The 5. Kompanie, positioned along the northern edge of the historic center, had to overcome strong resistance and moved into the buildings on the north-east side of the castle: connection with the 8 was made. Kp., already stationed at the edge of the gardens in front of the castle, the encirclement of the castle could be said to be

The Axis Forces

During the fighting a paratrooper observes the Italian positions: in the background you can see the imposing size of the ONMI building (Bundesarchiv).

While the clashes are still ongoing, Italian soldiers surrender to the German paratroopers (Bundesarchiv).

complete. Having concentrated the fire on the windows of the castle, which forced the defenders to stay under cover and therefore reduce the volume of fire, three paratroopers daringly managed to deposit two explosive charges in front of the doors whose explosion, which occurred around 5.30 pm, led the garrison to surrender. A white flag appeared from the torn boards of the door, the paratroopers broke in and ran quickly to hoist the Reich flag on the tower and above all to look for Badoglio and Roatta! Great was their disappointment upon learning of their absence from the castle! It was the late afternoon of September 9th and the Germans noticed that their situation was becoming increasingly dangerous: any attempt to establish radio contact with the HQ of Student continued to fail and from above they could observe the forces of the "Piave" division who were crossing the Tiber and then heading towards Monterotondo, while towards Mentana they could observe movements of Italian troops: the hunters were about to become prey! At 5.00 in the morning of 9 September the CAM's HQ transmitted Roatta's order to the "Piave" to abandon all strongholds and move outside Rome to the Tivoli area. The commander of the "Piave", Gen. Tabellini, however, remained skeptical about this order and therefore ordered his units to be ready to move, without however yet carrying out any movement. At 9.00 the first news arrived of the parachutists' launch in Monterotondo and of the clashes involving strongpoint H of Osteria del Grillo. Therefore Tabellini, correctly believing that it was necessary to keep open the communication routes between the via Tiberina and the via Salaria and between this and the via Nomentana, necessary for the proposed transfer to the Tivoli area, ordered Gen. Pezzana, commander of the divisional infantry and responsible for the defensive sectors west of the Tiber, to reach strongpoint H and then continue towards Monterotondo to participate in the attack that the II/58th Rgt.Ftr. was about to lead starting from Mentana. This battalion, which with the 4th Btr. from 100/17 of the 20th Regiment. Art. constituted a tactical group under the command of Capt. De Flammineis and acted as a divisional reserve, received orders to move to Mentana and from there attack Monterotondo.

In the square in front of the Monterotondo station, the armored car with the license plate RE 151B is stopped and abandoned (Wolfgang Stocker/ECPAD).

A group of Italian prisoners walk with their hands up along the Via Salaria on the morning of September 9th, followed by German paratroopers (Author's collection).

A pincer maneuver by the "Piave" was therefore looming which would have left no escape for Gericke's battalion, trapped in Monterotondo and without contact with Student, who on the afternoon of 9 September was still unaware of the outcome of the airborne operation. Around 2.00 pm the convoy under the orders of Maj. Trombetta, commander of the I/57th and made up of the 1st, 3rd and 4th Company and the entire III

Group of 75/27s of the 20th Artillery Regiment, previously located in the strongholds on the Via Flaminia, he headed towards the Tiber with the task of unblocking the 2nd Company, which had been engaged in combat for some hours. Once the right Tiber bank had been secured, the attack began at 4.00 pm in the direction of the Grillo bridge, conducted by two platoons of the 1st Company. The clash between paratroopers and the 2nd Cp. was still in progress, so it was easy for the men of the 1st Cp. to locate the German positions and force the paratroopers to stop fighting and retreat, leaving 4 prisoners in Italian hands.

September 1943: in the Regia Aeronautica barracks of Monterotondo Scalo, material abandoned by the Italians including three 65/17 cannons (Eugen Gremalsbacher/ECPAD).

Shortly afterwards the rest of Pezzana's forces, i.e. the remaining units of the 57th Rgt.Ftr. under the command of Col. Ferrara, the AT Bataillon and two groups of the 20th Regiment. Art., arrived at Ponte del Grillo coming from Prima Porta. After a quick COs report, Pezzana ordered the action to continue towards the Monterotondo station with the I/57th in the vanguard position. Trombetta put the 3rd Cp in charge. to rake the area between the bend of the Tiber and the via Salaria. The movement began around 7.30 pm: the onset of darkness, the uncertainty about the enemy's positions and the difficult terrain, well exploited by the paratroopers for sudden fire actions, slowed down the progression, so much so that at 9.00 pm Trombetta ordered the 1st Cp. to be a backup to the 3rd Cp. The advance continued slowly until a large building was identified in which the paratroopers had concentrated the Italian prisoners captured during the morning's fighting. Two attempts by the Italian infantrymen were necessary to dislodge the paratroopers, who retreated to the heights abandoning an anti-tank piece, but after overcoming this last resistance and having freed the approximately 200 Italian prisoners, the "Piave" troops were finally able to reach the station of Monterotondo, where they stopped to spend the few remaining night hours. At 3.30 pm the Tactical Group of the

II/58th Ftr. Rgt. reached the unloading area west of Mentana: De Flammineis deployed the 5th Cp. straddling Via Nomentana and the 6th Cp. to its left, each reinforced by a machine gun platoon of the 8th Cp., with the 7th Cp. as backup, the 100/17 battery deployed at the northern limit of Mentana, about a kilometer as the crow flies from Monterotondo.

Fallschirmjäger marching through the streets of Monterotondo, watched with curiosity by some Italian women, September 1943 (Bundesarchiv).

A German paratrooper in Monterotondo.

The objective was the first houses of Monterotondo, which coincided with the defensive line of the German 8. Kompanie. De Flammineis had to limit the use of artillery to avoid losses among the civilian population, therefore the 4th/II/20th fired a total of just eight shots, and only on clearly identified German positions. Despite the fire reaction from the paratroopers, the 6th Cp. reached the Radio Station of the Royal Navy, included in the German security line: attacked from three sides, the station was abandoned by the few paratroopers who occupied it. The 5th Cp. continued to move along the Via Nomentana in the direction of the town, hindered by German small arms and mortar fire. The next objective of the 6th Cp. it was the Capuchin Convent, seat of Gericke's command, but the high surrounding wall, well defended by paratroopers with automatic weapons, proved to be an insurmountable obstacle for the Italian infantry without artillery support. However, the situation was becoming increasingly serious for the Germans and reinforcements were sent from the Orsini castle, where the fighting was waning, to strengthen the defenses along the Via Nomentana which were put to the test by the attack of the 5th Cp. In the late afternoon, support was added from PAI (Polizia dell'Africa italiana) units belonging to the "Cheren" Column, Btg. "Bòttego", arrived in Monterotondo from Tivoli, where she had gone that same morning: there she had found Col. Montezemolo who, after speaking with the garrison of the Orsini castle, had ordered Col. Toscano, commander of the column, to take to Monterotondo to unlock the castle. The "Bòttego" arrived in Mentana between 4.00 pm and 5.00 pm.

Italian civilians surrender to German paratroopers in Monterotondo (Bundesarchiv).

Toscano found the "Piave" tactical group there which had already begun the attack on Monterotondo and, having approved the provisions given by De Flammineis, he made his units available to him. The PAI units, however, did not give an important contribution to the fighting: the tank company, with 8 L.6/40 tanks, showed little bite and incompetence so much so that its advance in the direction of the Convent was immediately interrupted, the motorized companies remained behind the "Piave" infantry without giving them any fire support and only the armored car company carried out exploratory attacks, reaching the point of making contact with De Renzi at Villa Federici. The only positive effect of the PAI's intervention was that its entry into combat was noticed by the Germans: realizing the numerical superiority of the Italian troops, Gericke recognized the danger of the situation and decided to try everything possible to get out of the trap that was closing on his battalion. He then ordered his senior adjutant, Leutnant Christiansen, to parley with the Italian troops at Mentana in order to gain time and try to gain information on the situation in Rome. He then approached the positions of the II/58th from where he was placed under the command of Col. Toscano as the highest ranking officer. The German attempted a bluff by even asking for the surrender of the Italian units, but Toscano responded harshly by highlighting that the Italian units would continue their attack and that there would be no escape for the paratroopers.

German paratroopers inside the town group together civilians among whom there are probably soldiers of the Royal Army (Bundesarchiv).

Il colonnello Edmondo De Renzi (Courtesy De Renzi Family).

In those moments, however, German planes flew over Mentana and the event was cleverly exploited by Christiansen who stated that Luftwaffe air attacks would be carried out shortly thereafter and asked to get in touch with the HQ of Student in Frascati. Toscano, impressed, agreed and therefore Christiansen, despite not being able to speak to the German command, managed to make Student aware of the critical situation of the battalion. The need to quickly resolve the situation in Monterotondo led to the stipulation of a truce agreement already in the early stages of the negotiations started in Frascati between the CAM HQ and Feldmarschall Kesselring: the Italian command was in fact urgently needed to unblock Monterotondo and allow the "Piave" to reach Tivoli, while for the Germans it was a priority to remove the II./FJR 6 from the dangerous situation in which it found itself. Therefore, when Toscano consulted Col. Montezemolo, who was aware of the ongoing negotiations, he confirmed that the II./6 should be left free to leave Monterotondo. A sort of "implementation agreement", with content in line with the main agreement stipulated between the CAM and Kesselring, was therefore confirmed in Monterotondo on 10 September 1943 and signed by Gericke and Angelini. The entry into force of the truce was set at 6.00 am of September 10.

September 10

After the night break, at 6.00 am on the 10th the I/57th resumed the attack in the direction of Monterotondo. The 1st and 3rd Companies and the regimental scouting platoon leading the advance left their positions close to the station and began to advance along the Via Nomentana. The morale of the infantrymen was high and the advance proceeded quickly until they came into contact with some paratroopers who remained to guard the access to the town. However, the Italian infantrymen, unaware of the truce, opened fire as soon as they came into contact with the paratroopers and the fighting immediately developed in confused way until, a few minutes later, Gen. Pezzana was notified via radio of the ceasefire. At dawn on 10 September the situation of Col. De Renzi's group at Villa Federici was critical: ammunition was running low and there was a shortage of food.

Oberleutnant Nitzschke and Leutnant Gustav Schiedewitz consulting a map (BA).

Believing that hostilities were still ongoing, De Renzi decided to abandon Villa Federici and transfer his men to Monte Oliveto to the positions of the 2nd Btr. 90/53 to continue the fight, but when he arrived there he learned of the truce of arms. Once hostilities ceased, on the morning of 10 September Col. Ferrara and Gen. Pezzana met Gericke to implement the agreements: the captured war material was exchanged, the prisoners were released and the search for KIA and WIA on the battlefiels was performed. In the afternoon the "Piave" column continued its movement through Monterotondo while the paratroopers were picked up on the 11th by trucks sent by the XI. Flieger-Korps.

Around September 17, Walter Gericke awarded the awards for valor to the paratroopers who had distinguished themselves most during the fighting in Monterotondo (Bundesarchiv).

Another moment of the delivery of decorations to the German soldiers which took place in Rome (BA).

Despite De Renzi's attempts to keep his men in his grip, the sight of the thousands of stragglers coming from Rome on the Via Salaria caused the morale of the soldiers of the "Re" to collapse and on 11 September the regiment had to be disbanded. On 11 September Col. Angelini called an official report from the units under him, at the end of which he left Monterotondo, thus starting the dissolution of the Garrison units.

The combat losses

The Germans had 54 dead and 75 wounded, therefore losses equal to 20% of the force that launched itself on Monterotondo. The paratroopers spent 10 and 11 September searching for their dead and took care of their burial in the municipal cemetery in single graves and provided with complete data of the fallen. Unfortunately, the treatment of the Italian fallen by their fellow soldiers was very different, so much so that to this day it is not possible to have an exact picture of the Italian losses: it was possible to obtain a list, unfortunately incomplete, of 122 Italian fallen, while at least 156 were injured. After the battle the Italian units also collected their dead, but without the necessary care. Apart from the "Piave", whose wounded were taken care of by the divisional health service and whose fallen were taken to the Verano Cemetery in Rome, the fallen of the other units were buried in the Monterotondo cemetery "in bulk", as already communicated by a few months later by the municipality of Monterotondo in response to the requests of the relatives of the fallen: "The corpses, scattered in various points of the territory of this Municipality, were collected by the military authorities and transported to the local cemetery where they were buried in bulk and without coffins in a mass grave". The Italian fallen therefore received disconcerting treatment: just like the paratroopers, the Italian commands also had the time and opportunity to identify and give a worthy burial to the fallen. The Italian officers, however, ordered the burial of the bodies "in a mass grave" without any apparent justifiable reason and without worrying too much about identifying the KIAs, thus failing in their duties as officers, soldiers and citizens and, acting with carelessness and superficiality, grossly disrespected their fallen comrades and their families. An often repeated question regarding the events narrated is "Who won?". Especially in local publications, the belief of a "surrender" of the paratroopers is well rooted, which however, as seen, did not take place, and therefore of an Italian victory. The answer to the question is simple, as it is sufficient to note which of the two contenders has achieved their objective: since these are diametrically opposed objectives, the achievement of one necessarily entails the failure of the other, there can be no doubt whatsoever. The aim of the paratroopers was to occupy the Orsini castle, while that of the Italians was to defend it. Gericke and his 650 soldiers in about 9 hours of fighting routed a garrison 4 times as numerous and reached the objective, unlike the defenders, and therefore there is no doubt that it was they who achieved the victory. Furthermore, almost all of the defenders, around 2500 men, were captured by the paratroopers, so there can be no doubt about the answer to be given to the question "who won?", unless we want to distort reality in favor of more or less ramshackle aimed at the use and consumption of their own political visions. This brilliant result was achieved thanks to surprise and speed of execution, the result of perfect training and careful planning which made it possible to overcome unforeseen difficulties such as the incorrect launch zone of half of the attack force and the casual presence in Monterotondo of forces equal to approximately two Italian infantry companies. However, chance also gave the attackers a hand: the Italian forces were caught in a phase of relaxation following a night spent in the complicated and laborious procedures for transferring the SMRE offices to Rome. The garrison was incomplete and the security measures had been relaxed for the good reason that their reason for being there no longer existed as the SMRE was no longer present in the town. Furthermore, two companies of the Assault Battalion, the most efficient nucleus of the Italian garrison, were absent because they left for Rome, leaving the defensive forces seriously impaired. The final question to ask is why such a bloody battle took place to conquer a building that was practically empty and devoid of any practical meaning. The responsibility falls entirely on the General Student who conceived the operation. With the collaboration of the German police forces, well present in Rome, it should not have been difficult for him to get an exact idea of what the Italian decision-making nerve centers were, but among many possible objectives, one of the least paying ones was chosen. In fact, the hypothesis of capturing Roatta or Badoglio in Monterotondo was unrealistic, as they should have been searched for in some Roman palace, seat of government and not in Monterotondo. In partial justification of Student, it must be said that the behavior of the Italian military leaders was so surprising, obviously in a negative way, that it was unpredictable and unsettling for those who, like Student and the German commands in general, reasoned in logical terms. In fact, no one could have ever imagined that not even twelve hours after the declaration of armistice on the radio, the main Italian military leaders, instead of being in their positions of responsibility, were fleeing towards Pescara following the King and Marshal Badoglio! It is sad to note, once again, that the Italian military apparatus paralyzed itself, due to the shameful escape of the military leaders of the three arms. An unimaginable behavior, so outside the logical schemes and the most elementary military principles as to be completely unpredictable for the now former ally.

Bibliography and sources

Archives

Archivio Ufficio Storico Stato Maggiore Esercito, Rome:
M4, b. 5
M7, b. 487
N1-11, b. 3004, 3010, 3014

Archivio Ufficio Storico Carabinieri, Rome: 1270.9

Bundesarchiv Militärarchiv, Freiburg:
RL 2 – III, Aktenband 1193
RL 33, Aktenband 148

Archivio Comunale di Monterotondo, Carteggio, B 68

Books

Mario Arpaja, ...attraverso la bufera, verso la luce – Diario di un Fante del 57° Fanteria Motorizzato, Divisione "Piave", Tipografia Regionale, Roma, 1948
Gastone Breccia, Nei secoli fedele – Le battaglie dei carabinieri 1814-2014, Mondadori, 2014.
Dietrich Brehde, Der blaue Komet, Schild Verlag GmbH, München, 1988
Enzo Cataldi e Roberto Di Nardo, La difesa di Roma e i Granatieri di Sardegna nel settembre 1943, Centro Studi dell'Associazione Nazionale Granatieri di Sardegna, Roma, 1993, p
Walter Gericke, Sprungeinsatz auf das feindliche Oberkommando Monterotondo, Der Deutsche Fallschirmjäger, 1953
Hermann Götzel, Generaloberst Kurt Student und seine Fallschirmjäger, Podzun-Pallas-Verlag, Friedberg, 1980
B. Pafi, B. Benvenuti, Roma in Guerra, Edizioni Oberon
Hans-Martin Stimpel, Die deutsche Fallschirmtruppe 1942-45. Einsätze auf Kriegsschauplätzen im Süden, Verlag E.S. Mittler & Sohn GmbH, Hamburg, 1998

Witness' reports

Report of veteran Lorenzo Fiorini, July 7, 2020

TITOLI PUBBLICATI - ALREADY PUBLISHING

www.ingramcontent.com/pod-product-compliance
Lightning Source LLC
LaVergne TN
LVHW081538070526
838199LV00056B/3705